中国思想文化术语多语种对外翻译
标准化建设项目成果

CHINESE THINKING AND CULTURE
MULTILINGUAL TERMINOLOGY DATABASE

中华源·河南故事
CHINESE CIVILIZATION
Stories from Henan

中原神话
MYTHS OF THE CENTRAL PLAINS

河南省人民政府外事办公室　编

·郑州·

图书在版编目（CIP）数据

中华源·河南故事．中原神话／河南省人民政府外事办公室编．－－郑州：河南大学出版社，2022.11
ISBN 978-7-5649-5351-5

Ⅰ．①中⋯ Ⅱ．①河⋯ Ⅲ．①地方文化－河南－通俗读物 ②神话－文学研究－中国－通俗读物 Ⅳ．① G127.61-49 ② I207.73-49

中国版本图书馆CIP数据核字（2022）第224060号

中原神话
ZHONGYUAN SHENHUA

责任编辑	陈晓林
责任校对	林方丽
封面设计	翟淼淼
版式设计	郭　灿
出版发行	河南大学出版社
	地　址：郑州市郑东新区商务外环中华大厦2401号　邮编：450046
	电　话：0371-86059701（营销部）
	0371-86059750（高等教育与职业教育分公司）
	网　址：hupress.henu.edu.cn
排　　版	河南大学出版社设计排版部
印　　刷	河南博雅彩印有限公司
版　　次	2022年11月第1版　　　印　次　2022年11月第1次印刷
开　　本	710 mm×1010 mm　1/16　印　张　10.75
字　　数	210千字　　　　　　　　定　价　55.00元

版权所有，侵权必究
本书如有印装质量问题，请与河南大学出版社营销部联系调换。

"中华源·河南故事"系列丛书编委会

顾　　问	黄友义　杨　平　范大祺
主　　任	梁杰一
副 主 任	卞　科　陈　岩　陈志伟　刁玉华　方启雄　韩国河 惠　康　焦开举　介晓磊　孔留安　李冰冰　李　俊 刘炯天　李向前　李　镇　梁留科　刘金锋　马萧林 牛书成　牛卫国　屈凌波　屈鹏飞　史永庆　田　凯 万正峰　王建修　王清义　王自文　许二平　杨建伟 杨玮斌　俞海洛　张改平　张俊峰　张明超　张松文 赵卫东
主　　编	梁杰一
副 主 编	李冰冰
编　　委	陈国良　陈　玮　丁　锐　高　阳　徐恒振　郑延保 孙立英　郭　远

中华源·河南故事·中原神话

主　　编	韩国河
副 主 编	罗家湘　钱建成
中文撰稿	刘玉叶　邵　杰
英文译者	贺爱平　姚源源　赵媛媛
英文审校	[美] Ronnie L. Littlejohn
绘　　图	严　琰　王梓若　吴姝然

The Editorial Committee
Chinese Civilization
Stories from Henan

Consultants	Huang Youyi Yang Ping Fan Daqi
Director	Liang Jieyi
Deputy Directors	Bian Ke Chen Yan Chen Zhiwei Diao Yuhua
	Fang Qixiong Han Guohe Hui Kang Jiao Kaiju
	Jie Xiaolei Kong Liu'an Li Bingbing Li Jun
	Liu Jiongtian Li Xiangqian Li Zhen Liang Liuke
	Liu Jinfeng Ma Xiaolin Niu Shucheng Niu Weiguo
	Qu Lingbo Qu Pengfei Shi Yongqing Tian Kai
	Wan Zhengfeng Wang Jianxiu Wang Qingyi Wang Ziwen
	Xu Erping Yang Jianwei Yang Weibin Yu Hailuo
	Zhang Gaiping Zhang Junfeng Zhang Mingchao
	Zhang Songwen Zhao Weidong
Chief Editor	Liang Jieyi
Deputy Chief Editor	Li Bingbing
Editors	Chen Guoliang Chen Wei Ding Rui Gao Yang
	Xu Hengzhen Zheng Yanbao Sun Liying Guo Yuan

Chinese Civilization
Stories from Henan
Myths of the Central Plains

Editor-in-Chief	Han Guohe
Associate Editors-in-Chief	Luo Jiaxiang Qian Jiancheng
Writers	Liu Yuye Shao Jie
Translators	He Aiping Yao Yuanyuan Zhao Yuanyuan
Translation Proofreader	Ronnie L. Littlejohn (U. S.)
Illustrators	Yan Yan Wang Ziruo Wu Shuran

总　序

中国是世界四大文明古国之一，也是世界上唯一的古代文明传统未曾中断的国家。河南省地处中国中东部，是中华文明和中华民族的重要发祥地，在中国五千年的文明史上，河南作为国家政治、经济、文化的中心就长达三千多年。从某种意义上讲，一部河南史就是半部中国史。这里是中华人文始祖黄帝的故乡，是古丝绸之路的东方起点，是少林功夫和陈氏太极的发源地，这里创建了中国历史上最早的都城，镌刻了中国最古老的文字，诞生了中国最初的商业文明。

伴随着新时代的荣光，河南经济社会发展迅速，人民生活水平显著提升，这是河南人民自力更生、艰苦奋斗的历史结果，也是对外开放带来的益处。河南经济社会的发展、人民生活方式的改变都植根于深层次的文化积淀。为了让世界更多地了解河南，让河南更好地走向世界，2018年以来，河南省人民政府外事办公室认真研析了这片古老土地上的历史文化资源和时代风貌，组织各领域权威专家学者，编译了"中华源·河南故事"中外文系列丛书，选取黄河文化、河洛文化、老子、庄子、黄帝、少林功夫、太极拳、中医、汉字、丝绸之路、古都、农业、大运河、文物、陶瓷、青铜器、手工艺、书法、杂技、豫菜、豫剧、脱贫攻坚、空中丝绸之路、航空城、南水北调、中原粮谷、红旗渠、焦裕禄等多个主题，力图以故事的方式向世界展现一个立体、全面、真实的河南。

当今世界，人类文明无论是在物质还是在精神方面都取得了巨大进步，特别是物质的极大丰富，这在古代世界是完全不能想象的。同时，当代人类也面临着许多突出的难题，比如，贫富差距持续扩大，物欲追求奢华无度，个人主义恶性膨胀，社会诚信不断消减，伦理道德每况愈下，人与自然关系日趋紧张，等等。要解决这些难题，不仅需要运用人类今天的智慧和力量，而且需要运用人类历史上积累和储存的智慧和力量。河南历史文化底蕴深厚，包容性强，在今天仍极具现实意义。中原文化蕴含的思想智慧有助于修身养性，推动人类社会进步发展，焦裕禄精神、红旗渠精神所体现的为民爱民、艰苦奋斗的价值取向是构建人类命运共同体的力量源泉。我们期待与读者们一起从河南故事中汲取更多的智慧和力量，共同创造更加美好的未来。

Series Foreword

China is one of the four ancient civilizations in the world, and is also the only country in the world where the ancient civilization has not been interrupted. Located in east-central China, Henan Province is an important cradle for the Chinese nation and Chinese civilization. In the course of the five thousand years of Chinese history, for more than three thousand years it served as the political, economic and cultural center of the country and therefore, as generally accepted, represents half of the history of China. Henan is the native place of Yellow Emperor, the cradle of Chinese culture, the starting point of the ancient Silk Road in the east, and the birthplace of Shaolin Kungfu and Chen-style Taijiquan—typical examples of the world-renowned Chinese martial arts. It was here that the earliest capital city in China was founded, the oldest Chinese characters engraved, and the earliest commerce took shape.

In the new era, Henan has witnessed rapid growth in its economy and remarkable improvement of people's living conditions owing to the national reform and opening-up policy and unremitting endeavors of the people. Modern economic achievements and social development as well as the changes of way of life could be traced back to its traditional values and cultural heritages. To enable people from other countries to understand Henan, and let the Province integrate more efficiently into the world development, the Foreign Affairs Office of the People's Government of Henan Province has organized teams of authoritative experts and scholars in relevant fields to compile this *Chinese Civilization: Stories from Henan* in Chinese and foreign languages since 2018 by crystallizing the excellence of traditions and outstanding features of modern development. The book series include *The Yellow River Culture*, *Heluo Culture*, *Laozi*, *Zhuangzi*, *The Yellow Emperor*, *Shaolin Kungfu*, *Taijiquan*, *Traditional Chinese Medicine*,

Chinese Characters, *The Silk Road*, *Ancient Chinese Capitals*, *Feeding the People—Agriculture*, *The Grand Canal*, *Cultural Heritage*, *Ceramic*, *Bronze*, *Handicraft Art*, *Calligraphy*, *Acrobatics*, *Henan Cuisine*, *Henan Opera*, *Poverty Alleviation*, *Silk Road in the Air*, *Zhengzhou—An Aviation City*, *South-to-North Water Diversion*, *Grain of the Central Plains*, *Man-Made River—Hongqiqu Canal*, *A Model Official—Jiao Yulu*, etc., presenting a panoramic picture of the Province.

In today's world, human civilization has made great progress in both material accumulation and ethical advancement, and the great abundance of materials today, especially, is beyond the imagination of the ancient people. At the same time, however, modern people are also confronted with a lot of problems, such as the widening gap between the rich and the poor, the indulgence in pursuit of luxury and extravagance, the undesirable extension of individualism, the decline of social integrity, and the increasingly tense relationship between man and nature. To solve the problems, we need to draw on the wisdom and powers developed today as well as those accumulated in the past. Henan is endowed with rich historical and cultural heritages characterized by its inclusiveness, and such heritages remain significant today. The intelligence and wisdom in Henan culture are conducive to self-cultivation and to the promotion of social development. The spirit of serving the people and relentless struggle, as embodied in Jiao Yulu and the man-made river—Hongqiqu Canal, provides source of strength for building a community with a shared future for mankind. It is our hope that wisdom and strength from Henan stories could lead us to a shared brilliant future.

前 言

每一个民族都有自己的神话故事，它们被人们一代代口耳相传，作为孩子们的睡前故事，舞台上精彩的戏剧表演，无数小说、影视的灵感来源，寄托着人们对祖先的无限想象。这些故事有些大胆奇幻而不着边际，有些听起来就像真实的历史。在数千年的讲述中，很多故事被作为真实的祖先事迹信奉，有的被收录进教材中。要认识一个民族的过去和未来，首先应当读一读这个民族的神话故事，本书讲的就是中原神话，也是关于中华民族的故事。

什么是"中原"？"中原"按字义来说，是"中部的平原"的意思。在中国，这是一个很复杂的地理概念，狭义的中原地区现在指中国的河南省，而历史上广义的大中原概念是指黄河中下游地区，除了河南，还包括山西、陕西和山东、河北、甘肃等省的一部分。这片大地被黄河冲刷，水土丰美，适合农耕，在这里最早耕种繁衍的就是华夏民族，他们创造了中国最早最发达的文明，他们的后代成为中国人民的主体。

"中原"还是一个精神性的概念，它指代着中国传统意义上最正统的文化。"中原"是中华民族的主要发源地，长期是中国政治、经济、文化的核心区域，在传统意义上几乎与中国文化等同。这种格局在中国最早的王朝——夏、商、周的时候就已经奠定，三代统治的核心区域都在洛阳附近，洛阳就是先民心目中的"天下之中"，最早意义的"中国"概念就是指代这片土地。如果我们再往前追溯到中原大地的神话时代，可以看到早于夏、商、周三代，那些中华始祖与中国文化的缔造者或出生发祥，或兴盛建都，或最后埋葬在中原土地上，率领中华祖先繁衍生息，使中华文明绽放第一缕光明。中华民族形成于此，中国人精神观念肇始于此，所以后世王朝"莫不以中原为正统"。

我们如果对比中原神话和古希腊神话，可以发现它们非常不同。首先，和古希腊神话以及世界上其他很多神话故事相比，中原神话没有系统宏伟的史诗，显得零碎又片段化；其次，和古希腊神话中各种神祇爱恨情仇的浪漫相比，中原神话里的神则显得相当正统而严肃，它们光明正大地出现在史书之中，人们往往将其作为写实的历史看待。正是因为有这样的特质，甚至在不到一百年前，还有一些学者认为中国根本就没有神话。

然而，这就是中原神话的独特之处。为什么会形成这样的特点呢？首先，有些专家认为，这和农耕民族的性格有关。中原大地水土肥沃，处于暖温带气候区，但是可以让人们几乎不付出任何劳动，就可以随手获取的野生果实却并不多，每个人都需要付出艰辛的劳作，才能将肚子填饱。所以农耕民族是一群每天都要早起晚归，侍弄那一片娇弱庄稼的人。他们非常勤劳，平时几乎没有空闲来高谈阔论；也相当谨慎，每天必须密切关注时令、气象，不让娇贵的庄稼死去。所以农耕民族是非常朴实、不爱幻想、脚踏实地的人群，故而他们的神话也不是天马行空的，而是和生活息息相关的。其次，这和中国传统儒家的主张有关，孔子说过，"子不语怪力乱神"，也是提醒大家专心做好眼前的事，而不是把自己的生命浪费在无谓的担忧和恐惧中。孔子主张每个人做的是"修身、齐家、治国、平天下"，这些都是利人利己的事。所以，中原神话中本来包含相当一部分奇特的、怪异的故事，都被后来秉承儒家思想的学者慢慢改造乃至舍弃，让我们现在不能看到原始神话的真面目了。

我们根据中原神话的内容可将其进行最粗略的分类，可以分为六大类：第一是创始神话，是先民对宇宙天地人类形成的想象，包括盘古、女娲、伏羲等神话；第二是圣王神话，是活动在中原地区的中华民族的先祖与文化创造者，包括炎帝、黄帝等神话；第三是英雄神话，主要反映活动在中原地区的传奇英雄，如后羿、夸父等；第四是自然神话，反映了先民对地理、日月、河海等的理解和想象；第五是神仙神话，这些仙人有相当多带有后代道教崇拜的色彩；第六是灵怪神话，是先民所崇拜的动物的变形，有神圣的图腾与吉祥的神兽等。这些在本书中都会有介绍。

当我们漫步在中原地区的城市中、田野间，还能看到不少当年神话故事留下的遗迹，可以称之为"神话遗址"。现在中原地区有"轩辕黄帝神话群""伏羲女娲神话群""大禹治水神话群"等规模宏大的文化群落。

轩辕黄帝神话群是与黄帝有关的神话遗迹，主要分布在豫西地区的灵宝、豫中的新密及新郑等地。例如，在河南灵宝，有传说黄帝铸造大鼎的地点铸鼎塬、有黄帝的衣冠冢"葬靴冢"，还有相传是黄帝所骑龙之须所化生的九孔莲藕。又如，新郑被称为"轩辕故里"。民间传说，黄帝的父亲叫公孙少典，母亲叫附宝，他们居住在新郑具茨山姬水河边的一个山洞里。附宝在野外感白光而孕，后生下肉团，黄帝从肉团中出世。后来，人们就将具茨山改名轩辕丘，在上面修了一座庙，叫轩辕黄帝庙。附宝感光受孕处有一块石头，人称天心石。黄帝成年后，四处寻找猛将良相，如力牧、大鸿、风后、常先、大隗等，这些人的名字成为今天这一地区的地名或山名。现在如果来到新密、新郑，还能看到当年黄帝留下的遗迹。

在今河南西华，可以看到传说女娲炼石补天所在的"思都岗"，现在还被称为女娲城；还有河南济源，地处太行山，太行山在历史上就被称为"女娲山"，也保存有女娲庙，最有名的是位于河南淮阳的太昊伏羲陵庙会，在每年农历的二月初二到三月初三举办，庙会上同时供奉"人祖爷"伏羲和"人祖奶奶"女娲。

又如，大禹治水的神话。现在来到中原地区，我们会发现很多以禹命名的地名，如河南省的禹州市，就是以大禹的名字来纪念他治水的丰功伟绩；河南的浚县，浚是"疏浚"的意思，也是为了纪念大禹治水疏导河流的事情。其他如登封嵩山的启母石、开封禹王台、桐柏禹王锁蛟井、三门峡等地的禹王庙，都会让人觉得那个神话的时代其实离我们也并不算遥远。

现在，我们来总结一下，产生于中原地区的神话的显著特征。

第一，中原神话体现了中原地区农耕文明的基本特征。中原先人对社会的理想追求是小国寡民的简单形态，对帝王政治的要求也是简单自然而不粗暴干涉，让每个人不误农时地耕作生活。对无为而治的圣王尧舜，人们衷心地唱道："日出而作，日入而息。凿井而饮，耕田而食。帝力于我何有哉？"重德重礼的价值取向从上古神话中就有明显体现。上古英雄人物往往都具备"父义、母慈、兄友、弟恭、子孝"的家庭伦理规范，我们都可以看到后世"父子有亲，君臣有义，夫妇有别，长幼有序，朋友有信"的儒家伦理道德观念的影子。神话传说在一般民众中起着宣扬人伦道德的教科书作用，也成为儒家思想的源头活水，滋养培育着中国人的生活理想与道德追求。

第二，中原神话中存在历史与神话的互渗现象，表现为历史的神话化与神话的历史化。古人都将三皇五帝、夏商周作为历史看待，而近代学术界掀起疑古风潮，怀疑周代之前都是神话故事而非信史，但近年来的考古发掘和"夏商周断代工程"都能够证明神话中相当一部分确实是真实历史的形象叙事再现。而且在传播发展过程中，神话与历史都在不断地衍变，历史人物越来越具有神性，如夏、商、周三代始祖的出生都成为感生神话，他们是被天神感召而降生的孩子，此为历史的神话化；与此同时神话人物也演变为英雄先祖及圣君而融入古史系统，当神话演变，主角都越来越脱离原始而富有人性，而且后来儒家的学者很多倾向于对神话进行理性化的解释，使神话成为历史的一部分。例如，史书记载，曾经有一个人就"黄帝四面"这句话，问孔子"为什么黄帝有四张脸呢？"孔子就回答："你理解错了，这句话的意思是黄帝选派能干的人去治理四面八方。"在这里，孔子有意将"四个面孔"和"四个方向"混淆在一起，将原本奇异的神话故事改造为正统的历史。人们感受到了越来越"像人"，也越来越像现代人的祖先形象，为之感动，把他们作为学习奋斗的对象，这在中原神话的古史神话中，体现得尤为明显。

第三，中原神话大多带有浓烈的英雄传奇色彩。一部中原神话史，其实就是一部远古英雄史。中原神话往往都是以神性的英雄为主角而展开的，这些神话英雄基本都具有氏族或部落联盟首领的性质，都做出了有利于人们的功业：或发明创造、改善民生，提高农业生产；或是文化的创造者，推进了民族文明的进步；或抗击自然灾难，挽救人民于水火（农耕社会中最令人恐惧的是水灾与旱灾）。这些传奇英雄都具备超凡神性，能使神祇妖鬼帮助，几乎是独自完成了改造征服的大业。民众更多的是仰望与依赖，将其转化为建庙、祭祀等的神灵崇拜。在中原传统观念中，人们多么期待一位圣王英雄能够救黎民于水火，承担文化、社会、政治各项功能，创造太平盛世。

第四，文化的多元融合造成了中原神话的丰富性与典型性。远古时代，来自各地的氏族争相逐鹿中原，苗蛮、东夷、华夏等不同的部落通过战争交汇融合，形成了以华夏族为主体的民族，不同氏族也带来了自己的神话传说，一并流传并积淀在这里成为中华民族的共同神话，这造成了中原神话丰富性与典型性的特点。往往一个原始神话有不同的情节展开与解说，也存在多个层次与叙述角度，今天看来依然残存着当初来自多个文化的神话兼容并蓄的痕迹。经过多氏族的筛选加工，流传下来的神话也具有更加典型的象征意义，层次更加鲜明，内容更加丰满，为我们了解当年多种文化的流徙与融合提供了极佳的研究材料。

神话是人类童年的梦境，美好、奇幻又捉摸不定，难以解释。那么，中原神话是中华民族童年时代对自然的认识与解释，是荒诞但又真实，杂乱却有秩序的梦境。下面，我们一起来了解这历史和梦幻杂糅的中原神话吧！

Preface

Every nation has its own tales and myths passed down from generation to generation as children's must-have bedtime stories, intriguing theatrical performances and inspiration for countless novels and films, embodying people's infinite imagination about their long-gone ancestors. With some seeming bold and fanciful and others sounding like factual historical events, many tales, in the course of retelling of thousands of years, have been recognized as true ancestral deeds and included in textbooks. To glimpse into a nation's past and future, one needs first to know about the tales and myths peculiar to its identity. As a repertoire of myths in the Central Plains, this book is also a collection of stories about the Chinese nation.

What does the concept of the Central Plains refer to? First and foremost, it should be understood as a geographical concept. In the literal sense, it refers to the vast plains in central China. As a complex geographical concept in China, in a narrow sense it can refer to the present-day Henan Province, while in the broad historical context it denotes the middle and lower reaches of the Yellow River including Henan Province as well as areas of other provinces in Shanxi, Shaanxi, Shandong, Hebei and Gansu. With the Yellow River running through it, the Central Plains boasts fertile soil and is suitable for farming. The first recorded people who toiled and multiplied here were the Huaxia people. They created the earliest and most developed ancient civilization in China, and their descendants have become the mainstay of the Chinese people.

The Central Plains is also a cultural concept, signifying the most orthodox Chinese culture in the traditional sense. The Central Plains, the birthplace of the Chinese nation, has long been regarded as the core area politically, economically and culturally in China, synonymous with the Chinese culture in the traditional sense. Its overwhelming importance was solidified in the earliest Chinese dynasties of Xia, Shang and Zhou, which all had their capitals near the city of Luoyang in Henan Province. Some historical facts placed Luoyang as the center of the world in Chinese ancestors' minds and identified the earliest concept of China as the Central Plains area. When looking back at the periods before the ancient dynasties of Xia, Shang and Zhou, we find that the Central Plains was a unique place where Chinese ancestors and the founding fathers of Chinese culture were born and buried. In these plains, they built capitals for dynasties, paved the way for the Chinese civilization to emerge and flourish and created the conditions for the Chinese people to multiply and prosper generation after generation. The Central Plains became the fertile land where the Chinese nation was born and to which Chinese people were emotionally attached, so all the succeeding dynasties took this area as the forefront of their reign.

A comparison between myths of the Central Plains and ancient Greek mythology will show drastic differences. First and foremost, in contrast to Greek mythology and myths originating in some other places, myths of the Central Plains appear to be fragmentary and lack systemic narratives or epics. Furthermore, unlike the deities immersed in romances and rivalry found in ancient Greek myths, the deities in myths of the Central Plains are rather orthodox and serious, even appearing in history books and being perceived as parts of real history. No wonder less than one century ago some scholars argued that there were no myths in China.

All this renders myths of the Central Plains unique. There are several reasons for this distinctiveness. Firstly, according to some scholars, the Central Plains myths are unique because of the character traits of its people who lived in an agricultural society. Located in the warm temperate climate zone, the Central Plains has fertile soil, but still it doesn't offer abundant wild fruits within easy reach. Ancient residents here had to toil and sweat in the fields in order to be properly fed, laboring diligently all day long caring for delicate crops. They were very hard-working, having little time for chatting or gossip; and they were also very cautious, paying close attention to the change of seasons and the weather every day to keep the fragile crops from withering. The farmers on the plains were very simple and down-to-earth, so their myths were not outlandish in nature but inextricably linked with real life. Second, the uniqueness of the myths of Henan's Central Plains was also influenced by China's distinctive Confucian philosophy. According to *Analects*, Confucius's disciples reported that he "always refused to talk of super natural phenomena; of extraordinary feats of strength; of crime of unnatural depravity of men; or of supernatural beings". Confucian teaching reminds people to focus on what directly concerns them rather than wasting their lives in unnecessary worries and fears. Confucius insisted that what everyone should do is "cultivating one's morality, raising one's family, helping run the country, and bringing peace to the world", all of which would benefit others and themselves. Therefore, quite a number of strange and weird stories originally appearing in the myths of the Central Plains were gradually transformed and even excluded by scholars following Confucian teachings, casting an opaque veil on the original colors of those myths.

The myths of the Central Plains can be roughly classified into six categories based on the themes of stories. Stories of the first category concern creation myths, which embody the imagination of ancient people offering explanations for the creation of the universe and humans, including myths about Pangu, Nüwa and Fuxi. The second category is composed of myths of ancient emperors about remote ancestors of the Chinese nation or the founding fathers of Chinese culture, including myths about the Yan Emperor and the Yellow Emperor. The third category contains myths of ancient heroes, which were mainly about the legendary heroes active in the Central Plains, such as Houyi and Kuafu. The fourth bracket consists of nature myths, which reflected ancient people's perceptions and imaginations about geography, the sun, moon, rivers and sea. The fifth group is devoted to myths of the immortals, many of whom were the targets for Taoist worship. The sixth category offers myths of the spirits and monsters which were transformed from animals and worshiped by ancient people, including myths of sacred totems and auspicious animals.

Strolling through the cities and fields of the Central Plains, one can still see many relics related to these myths, alternatively called mythology sites. In the Central Plains, there are now large mythology sites, including those devoted to Xuanyuan Huangdi, Fuxi & Nüwa , and Yu Taming the Flood.

As sites related to the Yellow Emperor (also called Huangdi), Xuanyuan Huangdi mythology sites now exist in some cities of Henan Province, mainly in Lingbao in western Henan, and Xinmi and Xinzheng in central Henan. Currently, in Lingbao City we can find a place called Zhuding Yuan (meaning the place for the Yellow Emperor to cast a tripod) and a cenotaph named Zangxue Zhong in memorial of the Yellow Emperor. Also legends associated with this place tell that the nine-hole lotus root was transformed from the beard of the dragon that the Yellow Emperor once rode. The city of Xinzheng is called "the Hometown of Xuanyuan". In the folk legends, Huangdi's father and mother were respectively named Gongsun Shaodian and Fubao, and they lived in a cave by the Ji River around Juci Mountain in Xinzheng. One day, Fubao became pregnant while walking in the country and seeing a beam of bright light. Later she delivered a ball of flesh from which the Yellow Emperor emerged. Therefore, Juci Mountain was renamed Xuanyuan Hill and on its summit a temple was built, which is now called Xuanyuan Huangdi Temple. The rock nearby where Fubao conceived is now called Tianxin Rock, meaning "the rock in the center of the world". When the Yellow Emperor reached adulthood, he went around seeking brave and wise men for help, such as Limu, Dahong, Fenghou, Changxian and Dakui. These names are now associated with places or mountains in these areas. At present, if you come to Xinmi City or Xinzheng City of Henan Province, you can easily find some sites and relics related to the Yellow Emperor.

In Xihua County of Henan Province, there is a place called Sidugang where according to legends Nüwa melted stones to mend the sky. This site is now called Nüwa City. In Jiyuan City, Henan Province located in the Taihang Mountains (which was historically first called Nüwa Mountain), there still remains a temple called Nüwa Temple. Interestingly, at the Taihao Fuxi Mausoleum temple fair annually held in Huaiyang of Henan Province from the second day of the second month to the third day of the third month of the lunar calendar, Fuxi and Nüwa have long been worshiped and offered sacrifices to honor them as the ancestral grandfather and the ancestral grandmother.

The same kind of folk worship is offered to Yu the Great who was credited for taming the floods. If you come to the Central Plains, you can find many places named after him. For example, the city of Yuzhou has its name in order to honor Yu's feats and accomplishments in subduing floods. Also the name "Xun County" is in remembrance of his success in dredging rivers, because the word "Xun" means dredging in Chinese. Some other places named after Yu the Great (also called Yuwang) include Qimu Rock (meaning the rock which Yu's wife turned into upon giving birth to his son). This site is located on Mount Song of Dengfeng City. There is also the Yuwang Pavilion in Kaifeng City, the Yuwang Suojiao Well (meaning the well for Yu the Great to imprison a dragon), and the Yuwang Temple in Sanmenxia City. These places can all remind us of our inseparable connection with those by-gone ages of the myths.

Now, with all this said, it is time to generalize the salient features of myths that originated in the Central Plains.

First, myths of the Central Plains embody the basic characteristics of the farming culture in the Central Plains. The ideal pursuit for our ancestors living in the Central Plains was a simple form of a small country with few people, and their requirements for imperial politics were also simple, preferring little brutal interference so that everyone would go on with their farming activities in perfect timing. They heartily praised the rule of the sage-emperors of Yao and Shun, who governed by noninterference, singing in their ballads of "Work at sunrise; rest at sunset. We dig wells to drink, and till fields to get fed. What is the emperor's power to me?" High values affixed to virtue and courtesy were also manifested in the myths where ancient heroes abided by the family ethics of "father being righteous, mother being kind, elder brother being friendly, younger brother being respectful and children being pious towards parents". These sentiments showed the early traces of Confucian ethics and moral concepts that "between father and son, there should be affection; between sovereign and ministers, righteousness; between husband and wife, attention to their separate roles; between the old and young, a proper order; and between friends, honor and trust". In this way, myths and legends functioned as though they were textbooks to promote human morality among the general public, and they became a source for Confucianism, nourishing the ideals and moral pursuits of the Chinese people.

Second, the myths of the Central Plains overlapped with historical records so that history became mythologized and myths embodied historical truths. Ancient people viewed the Three Sovereigns and Five Emperors along with the dynasties of Xia, Shang and Zhou as historical facts, while in modern academic circles there has emerged a wave of suspicion about the realities of antiquity, creating the suspicion that the reports of dynasties before the Zhou were a myth rather than real history. In recent years, however, archaeological excavations and the Xia-Shang-Zhou Dating Project have proven that a significant portion of ancient Chinese myths are indeed narrative recreations of real history. Moreover, in the process of transmission and development, myths and history are constantly evolving, and historical figures take on the characteristics of the divine. For example, the actual birth stories of the patriarchs of the Xia, Shang and Zhou dynasties have become myths portraying them as children born by the gods of heaven, making history mythologized. Likewise, mythological figures became a part of the records of heroic ancestors and saints, integrating them into the ancient history. As myths evolved, the figures in their tales became more human-like, conforming less to the original images. Later Confucian scholars tended to rationalize the details of the ancient myths, making them resemble a part of history. As recorded in history books, when he was once asked what "Huangdi of four faces" meant, Confucius clarified its meaning by replying that it indicated "Huangdi sending capable people to go in four directions to rule" instead of "Huangdi actually having four faces". Here Confucius deliberately juxtaposed "four faces" with "four directions", turning fanciful myths and legends into orthodox history. When mythological figures have become more human-like and been made to conform more to images of modern people's ancestors, we may be touched by their deeds and begin to worship and learn from them. This has become a salient feature of myths of ancient history in the Central Plains myths.

Third, most myths of the Central Plains have strong elements of heroic legends. A history of myths of the Central Plains is actually a history of ancient heroes. Myths of the Central Plains often took divine heroes as protagonists who were either leaders of clans or tribes accomplishing feats benefitting the people, making inventions that improved the people's livelihood and upgrading agricultural production. Or they were portrayed as the creators of culture advancing the Chinese civilization, or heroes fighting natural disasters and saving people from misery such as floods and droughts, which were greatly feared in an agricultural society. These mythological figures were portrayed with supernatural divinity, even to the point of being able to secure help from spirits and monsters, accomplishing unprecedented conquests and feats. They were the targets of worship and admiration by the general public and people built temples and offered sacrifices in their honor. In traditional belief, people living in the Central

Plains longed for a hero-emperor to deliver them from sufferings, meet their cultural, social and political expectations, and build a peaceful and prosperous world.

Fourth, the diverse fusion of cultures has resulted in the richness and peculiarity of the myths of the Central Plains. In ancient times, clans competed for the reign of the Central Plains, and different tribes, such as the Miao barbarians, the Dongyi people and the Huaxia people, fused through wars, forming a nation with the Huaxia people as the dominant group. With different clans contributing their own myths and legends, together they formed the common myths of the Chinese nation that have been passed down to the present, rendering myths of the Central Plains rich and unique. For any ancient myth one chooses, there are different plots and narratives interpreted from divergent perspectives, which still retain and display the traces of fusion and coexistence of myths from different cultural groups. Accordingly, the myths that have been passed down to the present are more symbolic, distinctive and richer in meanings, turning into excellent research materials by which to understand the evolution and integration of multiple cultures in ancient times.

Beautiful, fantastical and elusive, myths are the dreams of humans of the primitive period. Absurd but real, many-layered but orderly, myths of the Central Plains are a repertoire of ancient people's perceptions and interpretations of nature in the early days of the Chinese civilization. Let's savor these myths of the Central Plains and embark on a journey of history and fantasy!

目 录   Contents

第一章　创始神话　　　　　　　　　　　　001
　　盘古开天辟地　　　　　　　　　　　　002
　　女娲造人　　　　　　　　　　　　　　006
　　伏羲创八卦　　　　　　　　　　　　　012
　　燧人氏取火　　　　　　　　　　　　　018

Chapter 1　Creation Myths　　　　　　　001
　　Pangu Creating the World　　　　　　　003
　　Nüwa Creating Humans　　　　　　　　007
　　Fuxi Creating the Eight Trigrams　　　　013
　　Suirenshi Bringing Fire to Humans　　　019

第二章　圣王神话　　　　　　　　　　　　023
　　炎帝济世　　　　　　　　　　　　　　024
　　黄帝定华夏　　　　　　　　　　　　　028
　　涿鹿之战　　　　　　　　　　　　　　034
　　颛顼和帝喾　　　　　　　　　　　　　040
　　贤君唐尧　　　　　　　　　　　　　　044
　　德王虞舜　　　　　　　　　　　　　　048
　　大禹治水　　　　　　　　　　　　　　056

Chapter 2　Myths of Ancient Emperors　　023
　　The Yan Emperor Benefitting Mankind　　025
　　The Yellow Emperor Founding the Chinese Nation　　029
　　The Battle of Zhuolu　　　　　　　　　037
　　Zhuanxu and Emperor Ku　　　　　　　043
　　The Great Emperor Yao　　　　　　　　049

The Virtuous Emperor Shun	051
Emperor Yu Taming the Flood	057

第三章　英雄神话　063

后羿射日	064
夸父逐日	066
阏伯盗火	070

Chapter 3　Myths of Ancient Heroes　063

Houyi Shooting the Suns	065
Kuafu Chasing the Sun	067
Ebo Stealing Fire	071

第四章　自然神话　077

日月神话	078
嫦娥奔月	082
黄河神话	088
洛河神话	092

Chapter 4　Nature Myths　077

Myths of the Sun and the Moon	079
The Goddess Chang'e Flying to the Moon	083
The Myth of the Yellow River	089
The Myth of the Luohe River	093

第五章　神仙神话　101

共工触柱	102

蚕神嫘祖	106
地祇后土	110
玄女和素女	114

Chapter 5 Myths of the Immortals — 101

Gonggong Overturning the Pillar — 103
The Goddess of the Silkworm, Leizu — 107
The Goddess of Earth, Houtu — 111
Xuannü and Sunü — 115

第六章 灵怪神话 — 121

龙的神话 — 122
凤的神话 — 126
四灵神话 — 130
精卫神话 — 134

Chapter 6 Myths of the Spirits and Monsters — 121

The Myth of the Chinese Dragon — 123
The Myth of the Chinese Phoenix — 127
The Myth of the Four Spirits — 131
The Myth of Jingwei — 135

后记 — 140
Epilogue — 141

附录：中国历史年代简表 — 144
Appendix: A Brief Chronology of Chinese History — 144

第一章

创始神话

Chapter 1

Creation Myths

第一章 创始神话

盘古开天辟地

在古老的中原神话里，我们所居住的天、地的形成仰赖着一个伟大的神灵的创造。据说在天地还没有形成前，宇宙是黑暗、混沌、蒙昧的，天和地是连在一起的，就像一个大鸡蛋一样，里面分不清上下左右，也没有东西南北，但是，这个鸡蛋里孕育着一个生命，叫盘古。

盘古在这个大鸡蛋里酣睡着、生长着，积蓄着力量，他睡得很香，他就这样睡了不知多少万年。忽然有一天，他睁开了眼睛，发现四周是无边无际的黑暗，他想活动活动筋骨，可是鸡蛋壳紧紧地禁锢着他，让他动弹不得。盘古的心里一下子焦急起来，他从嘴里拔下来一颗牙齿，它一下子变成了一把威力巨大的神斧，他举起来对着黑暗猛地一劈，四周一声巨响，这个像鸡蛋一样的宇宙一下子裂开了。这一刻，被称为开天辟地。

天、地初分，在这个裂开的大鸡蛋里，那些轻而清的气慢慢地上升，变成了天；重而浑浊的气则慢慢地下沉，变成了地，从此世间一片光明。

盘古开心极了，他想要站起身来，可是天就像一个沉重的盖子压在他的头顶，于是，盘古就头顶着天脚踩着地，挺立于天地之间，努力地将天和地进一步撑开。自那以后，盘古的身体每天都要发生九次变化，每一次变化，他都会增高一丈，天也会随之升高一丈，地也随之加厚一丈。就这样，盘古的身体越来越高，天和地之间的距离也越来越大，天变得十分高，地也变得十分厚，这个巍峨的巨人就这样像柱子一样在天地之间矗立了一万八千年。

在这一万八千年里，盘古一刻都没有休息，就算是渴了饿了，也不吃东西，他孤独地撑在天地之间，心中只有一个信念：不能再让天地回到一片黑暗之中。终于，天和地之间的距离被固定了下来，可是盘古却已经精疲力竭，"轰"的一声，他倒下了，在他生命的最后时刻，他环

Pangu Creating the World

As recorded in ancient myths of the Central Plains, the formation of the world where we live was attributed to the creation of a great primordial deity. As legends went, before the formation of the heaven and earth the universe was dark, murky and chaotic. At that time, the heaven and the earth were connected together just like a big egg, and it was impossible to tell what lay upward or downward or distinguish where the four directions lay. However, this cosmic egg gave birth to a primordial being called Pangu.

Pangu slept soundly within this egg for tens of thousands of years, growing and building up strength. Suddenly, one day he opened his eyes but only to find himself enveloped in infinite darkness. He wanted to move his muscles and bones, but the eggshell held him tightly, preventing him from moving. Anxious to break away, Pangu pulled out one of his teeth, turned it into a powerful axe and slashed around in the darkness. All of a sudden, following a loud bang the egg-like universe split open. As the legend reports, this was the moment of Pangu separating the heaven and earth and creating the world.

With the universe splitting into halves from the cracked egg, the light and clear air slowly went up to turn into the sky, while the thick and muddy stuff slowly sank down to become the earth. From then on, the universe became clear and bright, no longer murky chaos.

Overjoyed, Pangu struggled to stand up, only to find the sky crushing on him like a heavy lid. He held up the sky with his hands and his feet were rooted on the earth. He tried hard to push the sky and earth further apart. From then on, his body grew nine times every day. Each time Pangu grew taller by about three meters, making the sky three meters higher and the earth three meters thicker each time. While Pangu grew taller and taller, the sky and the earth grew further apart, and this way Pangu stood like a giant pillar between the sky and the earth for 18,000 years.

All through these 18,000 years, Pangu pushed up the sky, never resting in spite of hunger and thirst. Heroically and alone, he stood upright, never letting the universe sink back into a murky lump of darkness. Ultimately the distance between the sky and the earth got fixed, but Pangu almost died from exhaustion.

顾四周,想着最后为这个世界做点什么。

于是,他最后呼出的一口气,变成了天上飘着的风和云;他最后发出的声音,变成了天空中隆隆作响的雷霆;他的左眼变成了光芒万丈的太阳,给人温暖;右眼变成了皎洁的月亮,点亮黑暗;他隆起的头部,变成了东岳泰山,脚变成了西岳华山,肚子变成了中岳嵩山,左臂变成了南岳衡山,右臂变成了北岳恒山,也就是现在的"五岳"。这五座大山耸立在大地的中心和四个角上,继续支撑着天空。

曾经在他身体中流淌的血液,变成了滔滔江水;暴露的筋脉,变成了纵横交错的道路;健硕的肌肉,变成了千里沃土;浓密的头发,变成了满天星辰;他的皮肤和汗毛,变成了花草树木;牙齿和骨骼变成了金属和石头;骨髓变成了珍珠;汗水变成了雨露。可以说,盘古在他生命的最后时刻,不仅创造了一个崭新的世界,而且把自己的一切都奉献给了那个只有天和地的世界。从那以后,天上有了日月星辰,地上有了山

Chapter 1 Creation Myths

He collapsed with one crashing sound. Toward the end of his life, he looked around, hoping to do something more for the world. And indeed he did it.

Upon his death, the last breath from his mouth turned into wind and clouds; the sound he made at the last moment became the rumbling thunder; his left eye became the radiant sun, shedding light and warmth; his right eye became the bright moon, lighting up the darkness. His bulging head became Mount Tai of the East, his feet became Mount Hua of the West, his belly became Mount Song of the Middle, his left arm became Mount Heng of the South, and his right arm became Mount Heng of the North. These mountains are now known collectively as the Five Mountains. These five mountains stand in the center and on the four corners of the earth, continuing to prop up the sky as Pangu once did before his death.

Meanwhile, the blood once running through Pangu's body turned into torrential rivers; his tendons and veins into crisscrossed roads; his robust muscles into vast expanses of fertile soil; his thick hair into stars; his skin and fine hair into flowers and trees; his teeth and bones into metal and stones; the marrow into pearls; and the sweat into rain. At the last moment of his life, Pangu not only created a brand new world, but also dedicated himself to the universe that once had been nothing except for the sky and earth. Thanks to him, the sun, the moon and stars appeared in the sky above, and mountains, forests, trees, flowers, lakes, rivers and sea appeared on the earth below.

About nine miles to the south of Biyang County, Zhumadian City, Henan Province, there stands Mount Pangu, which is said to be the place where Pangu separated the heaven and earth and created the world. Towering tall and upright, Mount Pangu boasts rugged rocks, lush trees and shifting clouds, where the enduring and touching stories about Pangu seem to come alive upon a visit. Close to Mount Pangu is the Pangu Temple, where a statue of Pangu about eleven feet tall sits gazing at people who come to pay their respects. Temple fairs are held twice a year on the third day of the third month, and the ninth day of the ninth month of the lunar calendar, during which many folk art activities are held, attracting throngs of visitors.

Pangu is acknowledged as the most primordial deity in Chinese legends and myths. Whenever telling a story about the earliest times, the old people in the

林树木、江河湖海。

在今天的河南省驻马店市泌阳县南三十里，有一座盘古山，传说这就是当年盘古开天辟地、造化万物的地方。盘古山巍峨挺拔、山石嶙峋、林木苍郁，在山峦之中，云雾缭绕下若隐若现的，是那个悠远而美丽的传说。盘古山的附近是盘古庙，高一丈零八寸的盘古坐像居于庙内，凝视着前来拜祭的人们。盘古庙每年都会举办两次庙会，分别在农历三月初三和九月初九，庙会期间会有很多的民间艺术活动聚集于此，十分热闹。

盘古，是中国神话传说中最原初的神。中原地区的老人们，想从最早的时候讲一个故事时，都会说："自从盘古开天辟地……"他是自然万物的化身，他用自己的生命演化出了一个美丽的、生机勃勃的世界。千百年来，中华民族在这片用盘古的血肉造就的土地上繁衍生息，盘古的故事也在这片土地上以诗歌、民谣、小说的形式被不断地传唱，延续至今，成了中华文化中一段脍炙人口的神话。

女娲造人

在中国人的心目中，有一位强大又慈爱的女神，她是人类最初的母亲。在中国南阳市的南关三皇庙内，有一幅石刻，刻的就是这位伟大女神——女娲。她长着人的脑袋，蛇的身体，梳着高高的发髻，手上拿着一株仙草。相传她对中华民族有三大贡献：一是抟土造人，二是设置婚姻，三是炼石补天。

第一大贡献是抟土造人，这在一本成书于战国时期的重要神话著作《山海经》中有所记载。这本书包含着关于上古地理、历史、神话、天文、动物、植物、医学、宗教以及人类学、民族学、海洋学和科技史等方面的诸多内容，是一部上古社会生活的百科全书。《山海经》中记载，女娲有一项神奇的技能，就是她能够化生万物，一天可以变化出70

Central Plains typically start the tale with the introduction, "After Pangu created the world..." He is the embodiment of all things in nature, exchanging his life for a beautiful and vibrant world. For thousands of years, the Chinese people have flourished on the land made of Pangu's flesh and blood, and the stories of Pangu have been continuously told to the present in poems, ballads and novels, becoming a popular myth in Chinese culture.

Nüwa Creating Humans

In the hearts of the Chinese there is a powerful and loving goddess who was the mother of mankind. In the Nanguan Three-emperor Temple in Nanyang City, there is a stone carving of this great mother goddess, Nüwa. She has a human face and a long serpentine body, wears a bun high, and holds a magical herbal branch in one hand. According to legends, she made three major contributions to the Chinese nation: shaping humans out of clay, initiating marriage and melting stones to patch the sky.

Nüwa's first feat of shaping humans from clay was recorded in *The Classic of Mountains and Seas* (also called *Shanhai Jing*). This book is an important mythological work written in the Warring States period. It is an encyclopedia of ancient society and life, covering a wide range of materials, including ancient geography, history, mythology, astronomy, animals, plants, medicine, religion, anthropology, ethnology, oceanography and the history of science and technology. As recorded in this book, Nüwa had a magic skill and could create up to 70 things out of nothing every day. After Pangu died from creating the world, there lived no life on the earth except for trees and flowers. Then Nüwa emerged and, seeing the desolate world around her, she decided to change it. She spent seven days in the first lunar month creating many creatures: the chicken on the first day; the dog on the second day; the sheep on the third day; the pig on the fourth day; the cow on the fifth day; and the horse on the sixth day. Thus six types of animals appeared in the world. On the seventh day, sitting by the river she shaped the mud and water into a clay figure exactly like her. Once she put the clay figure down, it began to move around and talk. Nüwa named this figure "Ren" (meaning humans). She worked tirelessly making more and more clay human figures, but she still felt it

样东西。传说盘古在开辟天地之后就死去了,那个时候天地之间空荡荡的,只有花草树木,没有一丝生机。女娲就是在这时来到了世界上,看到的就是这样一种荒凉的景象,她决定改变这一切。于是,她用7天时间进行创造:正月初一创造鸡,初二创造狗,初三创造羊,初四创造猪,初五创造牛,初六创造马。从此,世间有了六畜。初七那天,女娲创造了人。她坐在河边,用黄土和溪水照着自己的样子揉揉捏捏,捏出了一个自己。她把泥人放在地上,泥人不一会儿就动了起来,并且还咿咿呀呀地讲起话来,女娲把它称为"人"。她不辞辛苦地捏了一批又一批的泥人。后来,她觉得这样太慢了,便从崖壁上扯下一条枯藤,伸到泥潭之中,随后提起枯藤,向四处挥洒,只见泥点溅落的地方,都变成了一个个小人儿,这些小人儿奔跑在草原上、山林间、溪水中,大地上瞬间到处都有了人。但是,枯藤甩落时使用的力度是不一样的,所以造出来的人都不一样:有高的、有矮的,有胖的、有瘦的……也有人说,由于女娲是用泥土造人,所以她的子孙们都是黄色的皮肤。

第二大贡献是设置婚姻。慢慢地,女娲发现第一批造出来的人已经两鬓斑白,渐渐死去,难道要不停地创造人吗?有没有什么办法可以使人类延绵不绝呢?女娲想到了婚姻,她把这些人分为男人和女人,建立婚姻制度,让他们相互婚配,这样就能繁衍生息,世世代代地延续下去。女娲也因此成为中华民族的婚姻生育之神。

第三大贡献就是炼石补天。这在西汉皇族淮南王刘安及其门客收集史料集体编写而成的一部哲学著作《淮南子》中有详细的记载。传说,女娲造人之后的很多年里,天地之间十分平静祥和,她的儿女们也一直过着幸福美满的生活。可是有一天,水神共工因一次战争失败,一怒之下撞倒了不周山,没想到不周山竟然是用来撑天的柱子。天柱倒了,西北方向的半边天都坍塌了下来,天上出现许多大窟窿,地上也被震得都是深坑,洪水从地下喷涌而出,江河湖海的水也肆意泛滥,它们混杂着,泛起滚滚恶浪,到处是一片汪洋。山石撞击,森林中全是熊熊大

was not efficient enough. Pulling off a withered branch from the cliff, she dipped it into the mud and waved it around. Everywhere drops of splashed mud landed on the ground and turned into small man-like figures. They ran cheerfully among the grass, forests, mountains and streams, filling the ground with people. Some of these figures were tall, some short, some overweight, some thin, depending on how forcefully Nüwa waved the branch around to make them…According to some legends, Nüwa's descendants were yellow-skinned just because they were shaped from mud.

The second feat attributed to Nüwa was the establishment of marriage. Many years after the first batch of humans were created, Nüwa discovered to her dismay that these humans aged gradually and soon would die. She asked herself: Will I alone always have to create humans? Is there a permanent way for humans to last on the earth? An inspiration struck her and she thought of the idea of marriage. Dividing humans into men and women, she asked them to marry and reproduce so that human beings would last generation after generation. In this sense, Nüwa has been acknowledged as the goddess of marriage and fertility in the Chinese nation.

The third feat credited to Nüwa was melting stones to patch the sky, which was recorded in *Huainanzi,* a book of philosophy compiled by Liu An (the Magistrate of Huainan and also a royal family member in the Western Han Dynasty). Liu and his consultants based their work on a collection of historical records. Many years after Nüwa created humans, her human children lived peacefully and happily on the earth. However, when defeated in a battle with the fire god, the water god Gonggong bashed into the mythical Buzhou Mountain which was one of the four pillars to hold up the sky. As a result, the pillar of the sky collapsed and ripped open the sky. This in turn caused half the sky in the northwest to fall on the earth. The sky trembled and cracked open. Floods gushed out from the underground, and rivers, lakes and seas also flooded wantonly, turning everywhere into a vast ocean of fierce waves. Fire raged in the forests, and serpents and fierce beasts roamed rampantly everywhere. Many people were burnt, drowned, and devoured, sinking into the unprecedented catastrophic doom.

Seeing the suffering of her children, Nüwa was heartbroken and immediately decided to do something to save them and patch the split sky. She wondered what

火,毒蛇猛兽四处逃窜,人类面临着空前的巨大灾难。

女娲目睹这一浩劫,看着她的孩子们经受苦难,心痛不已,她决定想尽办法补天,拯救人类。可是用什么补天呢?女娲环顾四周,思索着,最终她在山上选取了各种各样的五色石头,用大火将它们熔化成石浆,然后用这些石浆将天上的一个个大窟窿填补好,自此天空中便出现了五色彩霞。

天虽然填补好了,但还有半边天空坍塌着,于是,女娲便斩杀了一只东海的大乌龟,她将乌龟的四只脚斩了下来,把它们当作四根柱子竖立在天空的西北部,将那坍塌的半边天支撑了起来。可是,由于龟腿太短,导致西北方向的天空偏低,天开始往西北方向倾斜,所以日月星辰都会朝着西北方向旋转,而大江大河都从西北滚滚流向东边。

为了让洪水不再漫延,女娲收集了许多芦草,把它们烧成灰,堵塞到洪水流经的大小沟壑中。女娲又举起顶天立地的长剑,赶走了所有毒蛇猛兽,将它们全都赶到深山之中,它们再也不敢到处祸害百姓了。

至此,人们终于从这场巨大的灾难之中解脱出来,天地之间有了日

she could use to mend the sky. Looking around and thinking hard, Nüwa finally came up with a plan. She collected stones of five colors in all sizes and melted them in the fire. Using the colored molten mixture, Nüwa patched the sky. From then on, clouds in five colors appeared in the sky.

When the sky was patched, half the sky still collapsed on the earth. Nüwa killed a giant turtle from the East Sea. The four legs of the turtle were cut off to be placed as pillars to hold up the collapsed sky in the northwest. According to legends, because the turtle legs were a bit short, the northwestern sky stood a bit lower and the sky tilted in that direction. As a consequence, the sun, the moon and stars also rotated in that direction while the water in rivers and lakes ran all the way from the northwest to the east.

To prevent floods from further raging, Nüwa burned a large quantity of reeds and stuffed them into the ravines and gullies where floods raged. Waving a long sword, she drove the threatening serpents and beasts into the depths of mountains, stopping them from attacking humans.

With humans saved from these unprecedented catastrophes, the natural rotation of the sun emerged. Then came the moon and stars, the change of four seasons in succession, the division of day and night, the peaceful flow of rivers, lakes and seas and ultimately a world of life and joy on the earth. Threatening birds and ferocious animals gradually became tamed and turned into friends of humans. Songs and laughter echoed in the sky and on the earth with the revival of life and rebirth of humans. To enable her children to enjoy their lives, Nüwa created a musical instrument called Shenghuang, which was made from gourds with 13 pipes inserted into it and shaped like the tail of a phoenix bird. When gently blown, it could make a pleasant sound. After making this instrument, Nüwa disappeared, never to be seen by anyone. In some versions of the myths about Nüwa, she was said to have died and been buried underground while in some other versions, she was said to roam happily in the world of the immortals.

Currently, there are Nüwa-related temples scattered in many places of China, such as the Wahuang Temple in Huozhou City of Shanxi Province, the Nüwa Temple in Tianshui City of Gansu Province, the Wahuang Temple in Hongtong County of Shanxi Province, the Nüwa Temple in Xihua County of Henan Province and the Wahuang Palace in Shexian County of Hebei Province. On the

月星辰的运转，有了春夏秋冬的更替，有了昼夜之分，有了江水河流的归顺，有了充满生机的乐土。飞禽走兽也慢慢变得性情温和，成为人类的好朋友，人们得到了重生，欢歌笑语再次回荡在天地之间。女娲为了让她的孩子们过得更欢乐，创造了一种名叫"笙簧"的乐器。这个乐器是用葫芦做的，里面插了13支管子，形状很像凤鸟的尾巴，轻轻一吹，就能发出悦耳的声音。做完这一切之后，女娲便消失了，再也没有人见过女娲的踪迹，有人说她长眠在地下，也有人说她遨游在仙界。

在中国的各地散布着很多的女娲神庙，如山西省霍州市的娲皇庙、甘肃省天水市的女娲庙、山西省洪洞县的娲皇庙、河南省西华县的女娲庙、河北省涉县的娲皇宫等等。传说每年的农历三月初一是女娲的诞辰，在这一天，女娲庙都会举行盛大的庙会。其中，河北省涉县的娲皇宫的庙会已经有1400年的历史了。河南省的西华县现流传很多关于女娲的传说与祭祀形式，如西华县聂堆镇思都岗村是传说中的女娲城，有女娲陵、女娲神庙。当地百姓每逢农历初一、十五就来朝拜祭祀，在腊月和正月举办庙会，唱大戏。中药黄芪在这里传说是女娲传给人们治病的，所以当地称黄芪为娲芪。另外，现在民间还有过天穿节、扫天娘娘、烙面饼抛在房顶上"补天"等习俗，是对女娲补天神话的再现与礼拜。

女娲是中华民族伟大的母亲，她慈祥地创造了人类，又勇敢地保护人类免受天灾。在中国五千年的历史上，中华民族遭遇了无数次的劫难，天灾人祸都没有打倒这个古老的民族，中华儿女总是能够如凤凰般劫后重生、痛定思痛、再造家园，这就是女娲带给我们的精神力量。

伏羲创八卦

传说伏羲是华夏文明的始祖，也是中国典籍中记载最早的君王之一。据说，有一个姑娘叫华胥，她外出游玩时偶然走到了一个叫雷泽的

first day of the third month of the lunar calendar, which was said to be Nüwa's birthday, temple fairs will be held in these temples. The temple fair, held in the Wahuang Palace in Shexian County of Hebei Province, boasts a history of more than 1400 years. Legends and worship rituals related to Nüwa can still be found in Xihua County of Henan Province, and particularly the Village of Sidugang in Xihua County which is alternatively nicknamed "Nüwa City" and where the Nüwa Mausoleum and the Nüwa Shrine can be found. At this place, local people will come to worship Nüwa on the first and fifteenth days of the lunar calendar, hold temple fairs on the twelfth and the first lunar months, and hold stage performances to pay her respects. According to local legends, Huangqi (a herb in traditional Chinese medicine) was used by Nüwa as medicine to treat humans. It became known as "Waqi" by the local people. At present, customs and practices reminding people of Nüwa's patching the sky can still be found in practices such as the Tian Chuan Festival, Sao Tian Empress (paper cuts in the image of Nüwa) and the custom of tossing pancakes upward to patch sky. All these folk forms are vivid reconstructions of the myth of Nüwa's patching the sky.

As the mother goddess of the Chinese nation, Nüwa created humans out of tender love and bravely protected them from catastrophes. In the course of history of five thousand years, the Chinese nation, battered by numerous wars and natural catastrophes, still stands on its feet and its people can rebuild their homes just like a phoenix rising from the ashes. Here perhaps lies the strength we can draw from Nüwa.

Fuxi Creating the Eight Trigrams

According to legends, Fuxi was the creator of Chinese civilization and one of the earliest rulers recorded in Chinese classical books. When a girl called Hua Xu went out to a place called Lei Ze, she saw a huge footprint on the ground and stepped on it out of curiosity. Miraculously, this made her pregnant and after 12 years of pregnancy she gave birth to Fuxi. It turned out that the footprint was left by the god of thunder who had a human head and the dragon's body. Looking like his father, Fuxi also had a human face and the body of a dragon.

Endowed with unusual wisdom and divine power, Fuxi became the ruler of a tribe when growing up. Back then ancient people made their living by hunting,

地方，看到地上有一个巨大的脚印，便好奇地上去踩一下，没想到竟然怀孕了，在怀胎12年之后生下一个儿子，就是伏羲。原来，这个脚印是巨人雷神留下的，这位雷神人头龙身，伏羲作为雷神的儿子，自然跟自己的父亲长得一样，也是人首龙身的模样。

伏羲拥有不同于常人的智慧和神力，长大后便成了部落的首领。那个时候，人们都是依靠打猎、捕鱼和采集野果为生，可是四季的更迭和频发的自然灾害使人们的食物来源不稳定，经常有人饿死，于是伏羲通过观察蜘蛛结网的方法，发明了最初的网，用网在水里捕鱼，在树林里捕鸟，大大地提高了捕食的成功率。他还教人们制造农具，开田种粮，这样人们不会因为食物的来源不稳定而饿肚子。

可是，在伏羲生活的远古时代，人们对大自然是一无所知的——天气为什么会变化？日月为什么会运转？人为什么会生老病死？所有这些现象，谁也不知道是怎么回事。人们遇到无法解答的问题，都去问伏羲，然而伏羲也回答不了，为此，人们总是每天提心吊胆地过日子。为了消除人们的担忧，伏羲经常环顾四方，揣摩着日月经天、斗转星移，猜想着大地寒暑、花开花落的变化规律。

有一天，伏羲在黄河边行走的时候，河水中突然泛起波涛，从水中钻出一头神兽。这头神兽头长得像龙，有角还有须，身体却像一匹马，还有密实且卷曲的鬃毛。它在水面上走来走去，如履平地，最后竟然走到了伏羲的面前，老老实实地站在那里一动不动。伏羲心里觉得奇怪，便仔细审视这头神兽，发现它的背上长有花纹：一六居下，二七居上，三八居左，四九居右，五十居中。伏羲赶紧在一片树叶上照着神兽背上的花纹画下来，他刚画完，那神兽便大叫一声腾空而起，转眼不见了，由于这神兽像龙又像马，伏羲就给它取名"龙马"。

伏羲对着"龙马"上的花纹整整研究了八八六十四天，在一番苦思冥想之后，他突然发现，自然万物均是由阴阳构成的。他根据"龙马"身上的纹样画出了八种图形，通过将阴和阳交替组合，并按照四面八方

fishing and gathering wild fruits, so the change of seasons and recurring natural disasters frequently deprived them of a stable source of food, often resulting in starvation and death. Watching how spiders caught prey, Fuxi invented the net to fish in rivers and catch birds in forests, making it easier to secure food. He also taught ancient people how to make farming tools and reclaim wastelands to cultivate. With the help of Fuxi, ancient people no longer suffered starvation for lack of adequate food.

In the days when Fuxi lived, ancient people knew little about nature. They were confused by many questions. Why is there the change of seasons? Why do the sun and moon move? Why do people live, get sick and die? They had no clues to answer these questions. Whenever questions arose, people would come to Fuxi for answers, which sometimes even eluded Fuxi, too. These unsolved questions sometimes kept ancient people worrying all the while. In an attempt to dispel people's worries, Fuxi looked around and pondered why the sun and moon came in succession, why stars appeared and disappeared regularly, why seasons rolled by, and why flowers blossomed and withered, guessing the rules guiding all these.

One day when Fuxi was walking by the Yellow River, a mythical animal whose head had horns and whisks just like a dragon's head and whose body was like that of a horse covered with thick and curly mane emerged from the surging waves. Riding the waves, the animal finally approached Fuxi and stood still. Hugely amazed, Fuxi examined it carefully and found some patterns in the shape of numbers on its back: one and six at the bottom, two and seven on the top, three and eight on the left, four and nine on the right, and five and ten in the middle. Fuxi hurriedly copied these patterns on a leaf. No sooner had he finished, than the animal sprang up and disappeared. Fuxi called this animal dragon-horse based on its resemblance to both a dragon and a horse.

Spending 64 days observing and pondering the patterns on the dragon-horse, Fuxi finally came to realize that all things in nature came from the combination of Yin and Yang. He drew eight signs based on the patterns from the dragon-horse, and finally he came up with the Eight Trigrams by putting these signs in eight directions in different combinations of Yin and Yang. The signs on the Eight Trigrams have different symbolic meanings in nature: Qian standing for the sky, Kun for the earth, Kan for water, Li for fire, Gen for mountains,

的顺序进行排列，"八卦图"应运而生。"八卦图"上的这八种符号包括了大自然中主要的事物，乾代表天，坤代表地，坎代表水，离代表火，艮代表山，震代表雷，巽代表风，兑代表泽，而这八种符号经过排列组合又能够指代天地万物。伏羲画八卦后，打开了人们理性思维的大门，人们的很多疑惑一下子消解了。同时，当时河洛一带的人们从伏羲那里学会了八卦，所以这一带的文化比其他地方的文化先进许多，而伏羲也因此被称为八卦祖师，博得了后人永生永世的怀念和尊敬。八卦中所蕴含的博大精深的文化内涵，成了中原文化哲学思想的标志，其无穷而神奇的奥妙，至今仍然吸引着中外无数的学者去探索和发现。

除了八卦，人们说伏羲还发明了琴和瑟，创造了乐曲，以用于礼仪、占卜、宗教、巫术等活动。伏羲的众多举措开启了人类最早的文化活动的先河，使先民从蛮荒时代转入了早期文明。同时，伏羲还集中了当时人们喜爱的几种动物的特征，创造了综合马头、鹿角、蛇身、鱼鳞、鹰爪等的综合体，称之为"龙"，从此，龙成了中华民族的图腾。

河南淮阳有一座太昊陵，这座陵始建于春秋年间，增制于盛唐，完善于明清，历史悠久，被视为"天下第一皇朝祖圣地"。当地从每年的农历二月初二直到三月初三，都要举行庙会，这期间每天都会有数十万人来参拜伏羲和女娲。2008年，太昊陵庙会以"单日参拜人数最多（约82.5万）的庙会"被载入了吉尼斯世界纪录，成为中国规模最大最古老的民间庙会。太昊陵庙会中保留了许多古老的神话遗存，如黑底彩绘的泥塑玩具"泥泥狗"，传说是古老的守陵神兽，还有当地妇女挑着花篮跳的"担经挑"舞，等等，都有重要的神话研究价值。

Zhen for thunder, Xun for wind, and Dui for rivers. These eight signs in different arrangements or combinations could stand for different things in the world. With the help of the Eight Trigrams, ancient people could find many clues to their puzzles, setting their rational thinking at work. At that time people living close to the Yellow and the Luohe rivers learned about the Eight Trigrams from Fuxi, and they soon developed a more advanced culture. Acknowledged as the creator of the Eight Trigrams, Fuxi earned enduring respect and admiration from future generations. The profound and rich cultural connotations in the Eight Trigrams are symbolic of the cultural and philosophical thoughts in the Central Plains, and these infinite wonders still attract countless scholars at home and abroad to explore and discover.

In addition to the discovery of the Eight Trigrams, the legends say that Fuxi also invented music and two musical instruments, the Qin and the Se for ceremonial and religions purposes and for divination and sorcery. These inventions credited to Fuxi helped to initiate the people's earliest cultural activities and brought ancient people into an early civilization out of their barbarian state. Combining features of some well-liked animals such as the horse's head, horns of deer, the body of snake, the scales of fish and the claws of eagle, Fuxi created a mythical animal and called it dragon. Since then, the dragon has become the totem of the Chinese nation.

The Taihao Mausoleum in Huaiyang County, Henan Province, which was built in the Spring and Autumn period, expanded in the Tang Dynasty and renovated in the Ming and Qing dynasties, boasts a long history and is regarded as the ancestral shrine of the first ruler of China. From the second day of the second lunar month until the third day of the third lunar month, a temple fair is held in the area, during which time hundreds of thousands of people come to worship Fuxi and Nüwa every day. In 2008, the temple fair of Taihao Mausoleum was entered into the Guinness World Records as "the temple fair with the largest number of worshippers (about 825,000) in a single day", making it the largest and oldest folk temple fair in China. During these temple fairs we can still see some traces of ancient myths which can lend important values for mythological research, such as the colorfully-painted clay dog which was said to be the mythical beast guarding ancient tombs and the dance performed by local women with flower baskets carried on a shoulder pole.

燧人氏取火

提起"火",在西方的神话中,不得不提的一位英雄就是普罗米修斯,他从太阳神阿波罗那里盗走火种送给人类,给人类带来了光明,但也因此受到了天神的处罚。而在中国的神话传说中,也有一位"普罗米修斯",他为九州之地带来了华夏之火,他的名字叫"燧人氏"。

据说,远古时期,中原大地仍是一片原始山林,燧人氏所带领的百姓就居住在这片山林之中。那个时候,人们主要是以打猎为生,但是因为没有火,都吃生肉、喝生血,这些食物不仅味道不好闻,还常常让人生病,很多人都因此丧命。有一次,山林中不知怎的突然烧起了大火,大火熄灭之后,树林中留下了很多被烧死的飞禽走兽,燧人氏捡起来尝了尝:"真香啊,比生肉好吃太多了!"于是,燧人氏马上带领大伙儿吃了这些烧熟的肉,生病的人大大减少了,但熟肉的数量毕竟有限,于是,燧人氏带领着大家到处找火。可是,他们翻遍了整个山林,脚底都磨出好多血泡,也没有找到火,燧人氏愁得坐立难安,天天唉声叹气。

突然有一天,一只浑身金黄的大鸟扑扇着翅膀落在了愁眉苦脸的燧人氏面前,大鸟说:"我知道你要找火,天上的太阳宫里就有火,我带你去找吧。"之后,大鸟把燧人氏带到了太阳宫,太阳宫的主人太阳公主对燧人氏说:"我听说你是一位非常伟大的人间首领,我这太阳宫里的宝贝你随便选,想要什么都可以拿去。"燧人氏看了看那些宝贝,摇了摇头,坚定地说:"公主,您的好意我心领了,但是我只要火,别的什么都不要。"太阳公主听后笑了笑,随手从地上捡了块石头,递给燧人氏,说:"好吧,我这里能生火的石头多的是,就给你一块,你回去吧。"燧人氏高高兴兴地捧过这块石头,向太阳公主道了谢,便骑上大鸟回到人间。

Suirenshi Bringing Fire to Humans

When speaking of fire, one would naturally think of the cultural hero in Western mythology by the name of Prometheus, who, in the act of stealing fire from Apollo, brought light to humans but received punishment from Zeus. In Chinese myths and legends, there is also a Prometheus figure named Suirenshi (literally meaning "Flint man") who brought fire to the ancient Chinese people.

According to the legends, in remote antiquity the Central Plains was dominated by primitive forests and there lived many people under the rule of Suirenshi. These ancient people relied on hunting for food and were forced to eat raw meat and drink animal blood for lack of fire. Of course the food was not delicious, and they always became ill or even died from eating uncooked food. One day a wildfire broke out in the forest and when the fire went out, it left behind burnt bodies of birds and animals scattered all round. Picking up one burnt piece, Suirenshi tasted it curiously and exclaimed, "How delicious! It is tastier than raw meat." Encouraged by Suirenshi, many people also ate the burnt meats and surprisingly fewer persons became ill. However, the burnt meats left after the forest fire were not sufficient enough for everyone, so Suirenshi and his men began to look everywhere for a way to produce fire. Searching through the forests and even getting their feet injured in the process, they still found no trace of fire. Disappointed and worried, Suirenshi sighed and became restless.

One day, suddenly a big golden bird fluttered its wings and landed in front of the sad-looking Suirenshi. The bird said, "I know you are looking for fire. There is fire in the Sun Palace in the heaven above. Just follow me." After that, the bird took Suirenshi to the Sun Palace. There the Sun Princess, the owner of the Sun Palace, said to Suirenshi, "I know that you are a very great ruler on the earth, so you may take whatever you want from the treasures in my palace." Glimpsing at those treasures, Suirenshi shook his head and replied firmly, "Thank you for your kindness, but I only want fire." Hearing this, the Sun Princess smiled, took one gemstone from the ground, and gave it to Suirenshi, saying, "Here I have plenty of stones from which to make fire. Take this as you desire!" Joyfully taking the gemstone, Suirenshi thanked the Sun Princess and left for the earth riding on the bird.

回到人间后，燧人氏立刻把石头供奉起来，焦急地等待着火的出现，可是时间一天天过去了，没有半点火出现，燧人氏气急败坏，对着宝石说："原来太阳公主在骗我，你这破宝石根本不能生出火来，那我还要你干什么？！"说完抓起石头，使劲地朝另一块石头砸去，只听"砰"的一声，火花顿时四散飞溅，惊得燧人氏当场一愣，"这是怎么回事？"他捡起了那块石头，思索着，突然，他灵光一现，明白过来，"原来只有用宝石击打石头，才能够生出火来呀！"随后，燧人氏用宝石击打石头试了好几次，看到每次都出现火苗，燧人氏才放下心来。

人们在燧人氏的帮助下，不用再吃生肉、喝生血了，饮食质量得到明显的改善，身体也比之前更加强壮。不仅如此，火的出现还给人们的生活带来了很多其他的好处，如帮助人们驱赶野兽，给人们带来光明和温暖，极大地提高了人们的生活水平。

在今天的河南省商丘市南三里，有一个高13.9米的大坟冢，据说这就是燧人氏的坟墓。人们为了表达对他的感激和尊敬，便修建了这座坟墓，以便世世代代怀念他，而关于燧人氏取火的故事，也从这片土地传播开来，成了一段脍炙人口的神话。

Upon his return, Suirenshi guarded the gemstone jealously and waited anxiously for fire to come out from it. However, no fire appeared although days after days passed. In a burst of anger, Suirenshi yelled at the gemstone, "Have I been fooled by the Sun Princess? No fire comes from you. Is there any damned reason to keep you?" Then he forcefully hurled the gemstone at the rocky ground. With one crashing sound, miraculously sparks appeared and flew in all directions. Greatly amazed, Suirenshi wondered why and how this happened. Picking up the gemstone, he pondered and pondered. Suddenly, a flash of inspiration struck him and he realized, "Fire can only be created by hitting a stone with the gemstone." Afterwards, Suirenshi tried several times hitting stones with the gemstone, fire came out every time, and Suirenshi was put at ease.

With Suirenshi's help, ancient people learned how to make fire, saying goodbye to the days of eating raw meat and drinking blood. With the improvement of food, people became stronger and healthier. Furthermore, the advent of fire brought many benefits to people's lives, helping to drive away wild animals, bringing light and warmth to people, and greatly improving their standard of living.

About 1.5 kilometers to the south of the present Shangqiu City, Henan Province, there is a large burial mound of 13.9 meters high, which is said to be the grave of Suirenshi. It was built out of gratitude to honor and remember Suirenshi. Today Chinese people still talk about this cultural hero and the story of Suirenshi's bringing fire to humans has spread far and wide, turning into an enduring popular myth.

第二章

圣王神话

Chapter 2

Myths of Ancient Emperors

炎帝济世

炎帝是中华民族的始祖之一，又称神农氏。很久之前，人们依然主要依靠打猎为生，偶尔也会采摘一些野果、挖一些野菜充饥，常常是吃完了这一顿，下一顿不知道要到什么时候，生活过得十分艰苦，而且人们也不知道哪些野菜能吃，哪些野菜不能吃，一不小心吃到毒草就会生病甚至死掉。人间常常闹大饥荒，饿殍遍野，大家经常会为争夺食物大打出手，人间如同炼狱。

相传，当时的炎帝还是天上的神，他不忍心看到人间这一切，决定下凡拯救人类，于是他化作一条赤龙，来到中原大地的上空，只见残阳如血的黄昏中，有一个女孩在姜水河畔踟蹰。那女孩感受到一道红光从天空深处射出，猛地一抬头，便看到了一条红色的神龙在她的头顶盘旋。那巨龙双目发出两道神光，跟自己四目对视，突然钻进了自己的身体里，女孩只觉头疼欲裂，而且腹中疼痛不已。待她稍稍缓过来的时候，夕阳已散，四周黑暗，天地间也没有了神龙的踪影。

原来，这女孩就是当时中原部落首领少典的妻子女登。女登回家后不久，就怀孕了，足月产下一个孩子。这孩子长着牛的脑袋，人的身体。他刚刚出生的时候，出生地周围瞬间涌现出了九口井眼，里面翻腾的全都是清澈的井水，而且这九口井的水是彼此相连的，无论在哪一口井中取水，其他八口井都会跟着波动起来。这个神异的孩子就是炎帝。

转眼间，炎帝长大了，他的父亲便将自己管理的部落一分为二，将黄河以南的领土交给炎帝管理，炎帝也因此成了黄河以南部落的首领。上任的第一天，他就把大家召集到一片土地上，召唤来一只遍体通红的大鸟，鸟的嘴里衔着一株九穗的禾苗，大鸟飞过天空，穗上的谷粒像下雨一样纷纷落到地上，炎帝让人们把这些谷粒种到土壤里。过段时间，土壤里长出五种不同的谷物，人吃了这些谷物不仅能够充饥，而且精神

The Yan Emperor Benefitting Mankind

The Yan Emperor (or Yandi) is one of the remote ancestors of the Chinese nation. He is also known as Shennong. In ancient times, people mainly depended on hunting for a living, and occasionally they would pick some wild fruits and vegetables as food. They lived a very hard life without knowing when and where the next meal would come. Being unable to distinguish between edible and poisonous plants in wild nature, people often became ill or died. There were frequent famines and deaths from starvation, and people often fought fiercely over food, turning the world into a hell on earth.

The Yan Emperor, who was said to be a deity of the heavenly court at that time, couldn't bear watching innocent people suffer and decided to save mankind. One day he transformed into a red dragon and came down to the Central Plains at sunset. At the moment of his descent, a girl was walking by the Jiang River. Startled by a red light shooting out from the sky above, the girl looked up and saw a divine red dragon hovering above her with two beams of light emitted from its eyes. The moment she looked into the dragon's eyes, magically the dragon went inside her, giving her a splitting headache and an acute lingering pain in her stomach. When she recovered, it was getting dark and the divine dragon was nowhere to be seen.

It turned out the girl was none other than Nüdeng, the wife of Shaodian (a tribal chief of the Central Plains). Not long after Nüdeng returned home from this encounter, she found herself pregnant and later gave birth to a child with the head of a bull and the body of a human. When the child was born, nine boreholes instantly sprang up around his birthplace. All of them bubbled with clear water, and the water from each of these nine wells was connected to the other. No matter from which well water was taken, the other eight wells would ripple likewise. This miraculous child was the legendary Yan Emperor.

When the child grew up, the Yan Emperor's father divided his tribe into two regions and gave the territory to the south of the Yellow River to his child, thus making the Yan Emperor the tribal leader there. On the first day of his appointment, the Yan Emperor called everyone to assemble and he summoned a big red bird with a seedling of nine ears of grain in its beak. When the bird

百倍，炎帝给这五种谷物分别起了名字，就是今天的稻、黍、麦、稷、菽，统称为五谷。

为了能更好地栽种五谷，炎帝开始制造农具，他砍了木料反复琢磨实验，终于制作出了人类历史上第一件农具——耒耜，随后他又做出了斧子、锄头、耙犁等用于开垦和耕作的农业生产工具，大大地提高了生产力。不仅如此，他还制作了陶罐、陶碗，方便人们使用和储存粮食。人们为了感谢炎帝教人种植五谷、使用农具的恩德，就将炎帝尊为神农。在今天的河南淮阳还建有神农五谷台，台内有神农殿，里面供奉的便是炎帝神农。

炎帝经常巡视四方，看到百姓大多深受疾病之苦，心中十分不安，就发誓要搜集天下所有能治病的草药。从那之后，炎帝经常在山间林中采摘各种花花草草，他有一条赭色的神鞭，只要那些花草经过神鞭的鞭笞，花草是不是有毒、属性如何都会通过颜色、形状的改变呈现出来。炎帝就通过这条神鞭，识别出了能够医治不同病症的药草，给人治病。

为了能够进一步识别药物的功能和性状，救死扶伤，炎帝决定亲自尝遍百草。有一天，他尝了一片鲜嫩的小绿叶，发现这种叶子泡水气味清新，还能够解百毒，他便把这叶子称作"茶"，随时随地带在身上，一旦不小心吃了毒草，他就赶紧喝茶，炎帝就这样把百草全都尝了一遍。在他尝百草期间，有时一天就中毒几十次。尝完百草后，炎帝便将草药按照温、凉、寒、热的特性逐一分类，还撰写了医书、药方，这就是中医的起源。现在河南省焦作市沁阳的神农山，传说就是当年神农尝百草的地方。

炎帝对中华民族的生存繁衍和发展壮大做出了重大的贡献，他运用自己的智慧提高了人们的生活水平，改进了人们的生产方式，得到了人们的敬仰和爱戴，越来越多的人前来归顺他。然而，炎帝一天天老去，他同一氏族的弟弟却在逐渐崛起，最终成长为了中原大地上另一个伟大的领袖——黄帝。

flew across the sky, drops of grain fell to the ground like rain. The Yan Emperor instructed people to sow these seeds into the soil. After some time, five different types of grain plants appeared in the soil. Eating these grains as food, people were no longer hungry and got stronger. The Yan Emperor gave different names to these five types of grain. They were: rice, wheat, millet, sorghum and bean. These are now collectively known as the five grains.

The Yan Emperor also put efforts into making farming tools to facilitate the planting of grains. After experimenting on wood for numerous times, he invented the first farming tool in human history called Leisi (a tilling tool and the predecessor of plough) and later he invented other tools for agricultural reclamation and cultivation, including axes, hoes and rakes, greatly improving productivity. Furthermore, he also made clay pots and bowls for people's daily use and storage. Indebted to the Yan Emperor's efforts to bring them five grains and farming tools, ancient people worshiped him and called him Shennong (literally meaning "Divine Farmer"). In present-day Huaiyang County of Henan Province, one can see the Shennong Five-grain Platform which houses the Shennong Hall dedicated to the Yan Emperor Shennong.

The compassionate Yan Emperor often went on inspection tours and was deeply bothered upon finding people plagued by illnesses. Determined to find as many curative herbs as possible, he frequently journeyed to the mountains and forests to locate medicinal flowers and plants. It is said that he had an ochre-colored divine whip by which he could tell whether the flowers and plants were poisonous, and what their properties would be like, just by observing the changes in colors and shapes produced by the lash of the divine whip on the flowers and plants. With the aid of this divine whip, the Yan Emperor could identify the right medical herbs for curing different illnesses.

To accurately identify the functions and properties of medical herbs for better curative purposes, the Yan Emperor even went a step further and decided to taste medical herbs for himself. One day, upon tasting a green leaf, he discovered that it left a refreshing smell in water and also could detoxify many poisons. Naming the leaf "tea", he carried it everywhere he went in case he might be poisoned by some unknown medical herbs. Trusting in his tea, he could taste as many herbs as possible. The legends report that in the course of tasting herbs he was poisoned by

黄帝定华夏

西汉时期著名历史学家司马迁的伟大著作《史记》，记载了从上古到西汉中期的历史。据《史记》记载，黄帝"姓公孙，名曰轩辕"，与炎帝是同一氏族的兄弟，他们二人都被认为是中华民族的始祖。当炎帝渐渐衰落之后，黄帝迅速崛起，并且很快成了中华大地新的主宰者。与炎帝相比，黄帝更加有才干，他一生曾出战53次，使得分散的各个部落逐渐走向了统一，把人们彻底地带出了蛮荒时代。中华民族历史上第一个共主的国家就是由黄帝创建的，正因为此，黄帝被称为"华夏始祖"。

黄帝的母亲叫附宝，也就是少典的妻子。有一天晚上，附宝正在院子里散步，看到北斗星枢星的周围有一道电光环绕着，电光绕着枢星转了整整一圈之后，枢星便降落到附宝的院子里，附宝便怀孕了。足足24个月之后的农历三月初三，天空突然出现了五彩祥云，一只凤凰在无数鸟儿的簇拥下飞到了附宝的身边，黄帝出生了。

黄帝自出生起，就显示出了他的与众不同，当其他婴儿还只知道啼哭的时候，黄帝就能够开口说话；当其他孩子咿呀学语的时候，他已经能出口成章；当其他孩子还在玩泥巴的时候，黄帝已经无所不通。黄帝的成长速度特别快，于是在黄帝15岁的时候，他的父亲少典便把自己属下的一半部落交给黄帝管理，让黄帝做了黄河以北的部落首领。从此以后，黄帝就带领着他的子民挖洞穴、筑房屋、捕鱼狩猎，人们的生活水平得到了很大的提高，许多部落纷纷来归附黄帝。

这个时候的炎帝年纪渐长，他看到原本依附于自己的部落转而归顺了自己的弟弟，特别生气，于是挥师北上，讨伐黄帝。炎帝的军队和黄帝的军队在阪泉之野相遇，他们展开了激战，《史记》中称为"阪泉之战"。这场战争持续了三天三夜，两军势均力敌，不相上下，征战卷起

medical herbs several dozen times even on the same day. Based on his first-hand experience, the Yan Emperor classified herbs according to their effects on the body, and also wrote medical books and gave prescriptions. His work later evolved into what is known as traditional Chinese medicine. Mount Shennong, located in Qinyang of Jiaozuo City of Henan Province, is said to be the exact place where the Yan Emperor Shennong tasted medical herbs.

The Yan Emperor made significant contributions to the survival and development of the Chinese people and used his wisdom to improve people's living standards and agricultural production. Widely respected and loved, more and more people came to submit to him in his era. However, with the Yan Emperor's aging day by day, his younger brother from the same clan gradually rose to become another great ruler of the Central Plains. This brother is later known as the Yellow Emperor (also called Huangdi).

The Yellow Emperor Founding the Chinese Nation

Shiji (*Records of the Grand Historian*), written by Sima Qian, the famous historian of the Western Han Dynasty, is a book of recorded Chinese history from antiquity to the mid-period of the Western Han Dynasty. As recorded in this book, the Yellow Emperor (also called Huangdi), whose family name was Gongsun and given name was Xuanyuan, and the Yan Emperor were brothers from the same clan. Both of them are considered the remote ancestors of the Chinese nation. With the dwindling influence of the Yan Emperor, the Yellow Emperor quickly gained in importance and became the new ruler of the Chinese nation. Unlike the Yan Emperor, the Yellow Emperor was more competent and aggressive. He fought 53 battles during his lifetime, gradually unifying the scattered tribes and leading people out of the barbaric way of life. The Yellow Emperor established the first unified nation in Chinese history and is thus revered as the remote ancestor of the Chinese nation.

The Yellow Emperor's mother and father were named Fubao and Shaodian respectively. One night, when strolling in the courtyard, Fubao caught sight of a light going around the Dubhe star of the Big Dipper constellation. When the light finished circling it, the Dubhe fell and landed in the yard, making Fubao

的尘土遮蔽了日月,死伤的士兵流出的血汇集成了河流,木棍等兵器都漂浮了起来。黄帝看着血流成河的战争场面,在军帐中对自己的将士们说:"原本就是亲兄弟,为什么要打仗啊?我该怎么做才能快点结束这场战争啊?"然后,黄帝找到了一只有双翼的神兽飞黄,黄帝骑着飞黄飞到了炎帝的军帐,见到炎帝便对他说:"炎帝,我的哥哥,我们是手足,是一家人啊,今后不要再相互打仗了。"炎帝听完之后也动容了,他们二人来到了父亲少典的墓前,想起父亲临终前对兄弟二人要"和睦相处"的嘱托,不禁悲从中来,抱头痛哭。从此,炎黄部落形成了坚实的联盟,炎黄逐渐融合,中原大地上形成了最大的部落联盟。

司马迁在《史记》中又记载了很多黄帝在和平时期的功绩,概括而言就是以德治天下。他教大家修盖房屋,发现了开掘水井的办法,解决了饮水问题;他继承炎帝大力发展农耕的传统,使得原始农业有了进一步的发展;他教导人们做事要尽心竭力,对于山林、沼泽、动植物的捕捉和采伐都要依据时令,有所节制。为了方便黄河两岸的交通,黄帝创造了船和车,给人们出行带来了很大便利;他的史官仓颉发明了文字,使人们结束了结绳记事的时代;他的臣子大挠建立了记录年月日时的天干地支的方法,创造了古代记录时间的体系;他的大臣们发明了上衣、裤子和鞋,人们从此再也不用穿兽衣树皮。黄帝还制定了国家的官员制度,并将全国分为九州来治;确定了天地万物的名称,划分出了二十八星宿;制定出有关生死的礼仪制度,让人们可以有序地开展生活。当时的人们已经懂得了音乐,黄帝让一个叫伶伦的乐师用竹子定下五音十二律,校正各种乐器,使得不同的乐器能够和谐地在一起演奏。黄帝还有一位叫岐伯的神医,是养生方面的专家,他的养生之术汇集在一起,最终形成一本中医学的基础理论著作《黄帝内经》。

黄帝在位期间,统一中原、奠定华夏、惜物爱民、政治安定、百姓和乐、文化进步,有许多的发明创造,并且形成了建立在农业文明基础上独特的中华文明。他建立了国家制度的雏形,使中国原始社会的发展

pregnant. Twenty-four months later, and on the third day of the third month of the lunar calendar, auspicious clouds of different colors appeared in the sky and a phoenix surrounded by numerous other birds flew over to Fubao. As this occurred, Fubao gave birth to the Yellow Emperor.

The Yellow Emperor distinguished himself from other children of his age and grew up more quickly. When other babies could only cry, he was able to speak; when other children were learning to speak, he could recite a lot; when other children were still interested in playing in the mud, he knew a vast amount and could do many things on his own. At fifteen, he was entrusted by his father (Shaodian) with the leadership of half of the old man's tribes and thus he became the ruler of the tribes to the north of the Yellow River. In his new role as ruler the Yellow Emperor led his tribesmen to dig caves, build houses, fish and hunt, and people's living standards were greatly improved, thereby attracting many tribes to join under his rule.

Seeing many of his former tribes switch allegiance to his young brother, the aging Yan Emperor got angry and launched a war against the Yellow Emperor to get back what had once belonged to him. The two armies fought fiercely in a place called Banquan, and this became known as "the Battle of Banquan" in *Shiji* (*Records of the Grand Historian*). The fight lasted three days and nights and the two armies were evenly matched. The dust from the battle blotted out the sun and moon, and blood from the dead and wounded soldiers gathered into rivers where the wooden sticks and other weapons also floated up. The Yellow Emperor, looking at the bloody scene, said to his generals in the military tent, "Why are we fighting when we are originally brothers? What can I do to end this war quickly?" Then the Yellow Emperor rode Feihuang, a divine beast with two wings, to the military tent of the Yan Emperor and said earnestly, "My brother, we are family with blood ties. Let's not fight each other like this." Hearing this, the Yan Emperor got deeply touched. Together they went to their father's tomb. Recalling their father's advice for them to live in harmony, they burst into tears and hugged each other tightly. Since then the tribes of the Yan Emperor and the Yellow Emperor made an alliance and integrated into the largest group of the Chinese people.

Shiji (*Records of the Grand Historian*), written by Sima Qian, recorded the

发生了历史性的飞跃,从野蛮时代,进入了初步的文明时代,揭开了中华文明历史的新篇章。黄帝出生和建都的地方即现在的河南省新郑市,古代官民为纪念黄帝的功业,在传说黄帝出生的轩辕丘旁建轩辕故里祠,又在黄帝建功立业的具茨山(今始祖山)风后顶之巅筑轩辕庙。自春秋时起,每年农历三月初三,当地的人们都要在轩辕庙、轩辕故里祠隆重举行拜祖庆典以示纪念,这种拜祖习俗一直延续至今,从未间断,寄托了中国人民对始祖黄帝的无限尊敬和想念。

另外,在河南灵宝的阳平镇,有传说黄帝铸鼎之处铸鼎塬。这里的传说反映了黄帝神话在后世传播的过程中逐渐染上道教神仙化的色彩。《山海经》中说此处山上多白玉,黄帝以此为食,并取其精华炼丹。黄帝还开采铜矿而炼鼎,鼎铸成后,有龙下迎,黄帝骑龙而去。传说中百姓因不舍而阻拦,拉扯掉黄帝的衣袖和靴子埋葬在这里,故而此地同黄陵县的桥山黄帝陵一样,也是黄帝的衣冠冢,民间也称"葬靴冢"。帝陵位于铸鼎塬之北,为黄土夯筑,高约6米,周长40余米,陵前原有汉武帝所建的黄帝庙,建筑基址尚存。黄帝陵西南有传说龙须掉落形成的龙须沟。此地对先祖黄帝的祭祀活动至今仍规模不减,每逢黄帝诞辰的农历三月初三,寻根问祖与祭祀拜谒的人络绎不绝,共同前来纪念这位华夏子孙的祖先!

Yellow Emperor's achievements and feats in times of peace during his governance by virtue. He taught people to build houses and discovered the method of digging wells to get drinking water. He carried forward the tradition of developing agriculture which had been first established by the Yan Emperor, greatly advancing primitive agriculture. He also taught people to be diligent in their work and be restrained in hunting animals and harvesting, paying attention to changes of seasons. Furthermore, the Yellow Emperor invented ships and carts to facilitate the transport along both sides of the Yellow River, making it convenient for people to travel. During his reign, Cangjie, one of the Yellow Emperor's ministers, invented writing and put an end to the practice of recording events by knotting ropes. Danao, another minister under the Yellow Emperor, invented the method of recording the year, month, day and hour by using the Ten Celestial Stems and the Twelve Terrestrial Branches. During the reign of the Yellow Emperor, jackets, trousers and shoes were invented and people no longer had to be clothed in animal fur or tree bark. The Yellow Emperor also established a system of state officials and divided the country into nine states to make ruling them more efficient. He determined names of all things in heaven and earth and divided the 28 stars and constellations. He developed a system of rituals concerning life and death so that people could conduct their lives in an orderly manner. At that time, people already knew about and played music, and a musician named Linglun used bamboo to set five tones and twelve rhythms for musical instruments so that different instruments could be played together in harmony. The Yellow Emperor also had a physician named Qibo, who was an expert in healthcare, and his techniques were brought together to form *Huangdi Neijing* (also called *The Inner Classic of the Yellow Emperor*), a medical book on basic theories of traditional Chinese medicine.

  During his reign, the Yellow Emperor unified the Central Plains, founded the Chinese nation, cherished resources, loved the people, forged political stability, and advanced the progress of Chinese culture, enabling people to live a happy life. In his time, many inventions emerged. The unique Chinese civilization based on agricultural economy also came into existence. He established the prototype of the state system and led people out of the barbaric society and into a preliminary civilized one, making a historic leap and opening a new chapter

涿鹿之战

涿鹿之战是华夏民族统一后的第一场也是最大的一场战争，这场史诗级的战争最终奠定了华夏部落在中原大地稳固的统治地位。

当时南方最强大的部落联盟是九黎部落，这是居住在今天长江一带的九个部落的联盟。九黎族的首领叫蚩尤，他一共有81个兄弟，个个都是铜头铁额，他们长相怪异，兽身人语，勇猛无比，以石头和沙子为食，特别擅长制造刀、弓箭、斧头、盾牌等武器。他们也试图占领地理位置居中、水草丰美的中原大地，企图"逐鹿中原"。

九黎部落一直向北推进，先与炎帝部落短兵相接。九黎部落战士凶猛，武器先进，炎帝部落节节败退，向黄帝部落求救。炎黄部落联合起来，集合了最强的战力，向蚩尤迎战。一场惊天动地的战争不可避免地在涿鹿爆发了。

《山海经》中记载，战争之初，是蚩尤占上风，连连取胜。黄帝请来了"雨水之神"应龙，应龙是一只带着翅膀的飞龙，只见他从口中吐出一条水柱，朝着蚩尤的士兵喷去，喷得他们摇摇晃晃，步步后退。蚩尤见状，忙从怀中掏出一个竹筒，对着天空连吹了三口气，不一会儿，雷电交加，"风神"风伯和"雨神"雨师从空中赶来，风伯用剑一指，顿时狂风大作，应龙喷出的水都被刮了回来，反刮到黄帝的军阵中，黄帝的士兵冷不丁被水喷到，纷纷后退，蚩尤的军队趁机又扑了上来。应龙不甘示弱，他双翅一展，飞上高空，口朝下喷，形成了一个水柱，像瀑布一样包围住蚩尤的部队，可是雨师只是挥了挥手指头，水柱立刻倾盆而落，并且很快汇集成江河，冲向黄帝的军阵，蚩尤也立刻乘胜追击，黄帝的军队大败而归。

就在黄帝想要退兵再议之时，从西北方向的天空中飞来了一位天女，这天女有一身漂亮的羽毛，她飞降到黄帝身边，对黄帝说："别

in the history of Chinese civilization. The place where the Yellow Emperor was born and built his capital is in the present-day Xinzheng City, Henan Province. To commemorate his achievements, people here built the Xuanyuan Ancestral Hall around the Xuanyuan Hill which is said to have been the Yellow Emperor's birthplace. They also built the Xuanyuan Temple on the summit of .Juci Mountain (i.e., the present-day Ancestor Mountain) which was said to be where the Yellow Emperor accomplished most of his achievements. Since the Spring and Autumn period, it was the custom every year on the third day of the third month of the lunar calendar for local people to hold a grand ancestral worship and celebration ceremony at the Xuanyuan Temple and the Xuanyuan Ancestral Hall to commemorate the Yellow Emperor. This custom of ancestral worship has continued uninterruptedly to this day and manifested the Chinese people's infinite respect and longing for their ancestor.

In the town of Yangping in Lingbao County, Henan Province, there is a place called Zhuding Yuan which is said to be the place where the Yellow Emperor cast the alchemical tripod. The legends about this act show that myths of the Yellow Emperor were gradually tinted over time with Taoist ideas. As recorded in *The Classic of Mountains and Seas*, the mountains in this area abounded with white jade, which was eaten by the Yellow Emperor as food and whose essence was extracted by him through alchemy to make pills. The Yellow Emperor mined copper to cast the tripod. After the tripod was finished, a dragon came down to meet him, and the Yellow Emperor rode away on the dragon. The legend reports that local people tried to stop him from leaving and pulled down his sleeves and boots, which were then buried in that place, forming another Cenotaph of the Yellow Emperor known as Zangxue Zhong, which was similar to the Huangdi Mausoleum in Huangling County. The Huangdi Mausoleum, located to the north of Zhuding Yuan, is a rammed loess structure with a height of about 6 meters and a circumference of more than 40 meters. In front of the mausoleum was the Emperor Temple built by Emperor Wu of the Han Dynasty, whose remaining relics are still preserved. To the southwest of the Huangdi Mausoleum, there is a legendary place called Long Xu Ditch ("Long" and "Xu" respectively mean the dragon and beard in Chinese) which was said to be formed by the dragon's falling beard. Here ceremonies and worship activities in honor of the Yellow Emperor

第二章　圣王神话

着急退兵，我能够破他的阵法。"说罢，她取出一把扇子，对着风雨一扇，风雨骤停；她又从翅膀上拔出一根羽毛，放在手掌上，那羽毛立刻化为一根火棍。刹那间，火棍由细变粗，发出一道巨光射向了风伯和雨师，蚩尤的兵将个个热得大汗淋漓，步履难行。这天女就是"旱神"女魃，一直居住在昆仑山上，听说黄帝有难，特地来帮助他。

蚩尤吃了败仗，终日抓耳挠腮，坐立不宁。突然，他有了主意，他让他的士兵去叫阵，然后佯装败退，把黄帝的军队引到一处山谷中，随后他站在山谷外，两手撑着一个大口袋，对着黄帝的军队喷雾，大雾弥

are still held on a large scale. On the third day of the third month of the lunar calendar which was said to be the Yellow Emperor's birthday, throngs of people would visit these places to worship and commemorate the Yellow Emperor, the remote ancestor of the Chinese nation.

The Battle of Zhuolu

The Battle of Zhuolu was the first and also the largest war in antiquity after the unification of the Chinese nation. This epic war finally established the stable dominance of the Huaxia tribes in the Central Plains.

At that time, the most powerful tribal alliance in the south was the Jiuli tribes, which consisted of nine tribes living along the present-day Yangtze River. Chiyou, the leader of the Jiuli tribes, had 81 brothers, all of whom had bizarre appearances with copper-like heads and iron-like foreheads. They spoke the human language but had beast-like bodies, full of valour and vigor. They fed on stones and sand and were quite adept at making weapons, especially knives, bows and arrows, axes, and shields. They, in an attempt to bid for state power, also tried to occupy the Central Plains, which was blessed with an advantageous geographical location, abundant water resources and lush grasses.

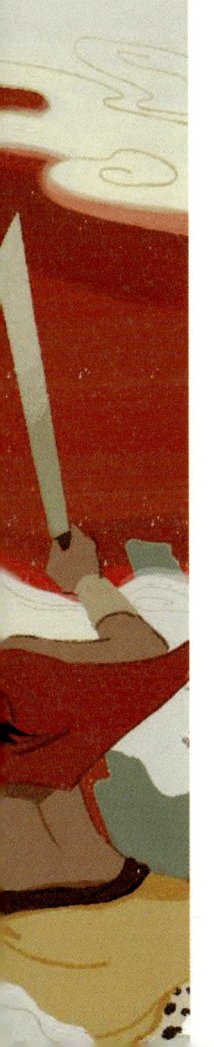

The Jiuli tribes kept advancing northwards and first came into close quarters against the Yan Emperor's tribe. Yan's group was steadily losing ground and had to turn to the Yellow Emperor's tribe for aid as the Jiuli tribes had fierce warriors and advanced weapons. The Yan Emperor's and the Yellow Emperor's tribes united and gathered the strongest fighting power of the Huaxia tribes to fight against Chiyou. An earth-shattering war inevitably broke out in Zhuolu.

According to *The Classic of Mountains and Seas*, in the beginning of the war, it was Chiyou who had the upper hand and won consecutive victories. Then the Yellow Emperor sought help from Yinglong, the God of Rain. Yinglong was a flying dragon with wings. He spat out a jet of water from his mouth and sprayed it towards Chiyou's soldiers, causing them to sway and step back. Seeing this, Chiyou hurriedly took out a bamboo tube from his arms and blew three breaths against the sky. Before long, with thunder and lightning following one another, Fengbo, the Wind God and Yushi, the Rain God came from the air. As

漫，黄帝的军队在漫天的雾中迷失了方向，士兵们乱作一团，踩踏声、惨叫声、呼救声不绝于耳。等完全听不见声音，蚩尤才收了口袋，大雾散去，尸横遍野，只有极少数的士兵存活了下来。黄帝的军队遭遇了灭顶之灾，他将自己整日锁在房间里，思考对策。一天，一只人头鸟身的女子落在了黄帝跟前，说："我是天上的九天玄女，知你有难，这本兵书就送给你吧！"黄帝谢过了九天玄女，仔细研读兵书后命人制造了12辆指南车，每个车上都有一个伸着手臂的小木人，不论车子如何运行，小木人的手总是指向南方。等蚩尤再次施放雾气的时候，黄帝的军队在指南车的帮助下冲出了大雾。

蚩尤使出了最后的撒手锏，他派出魑魅魍魉等一众鬼怪，它们不仅能够发出控制人神志的声音，还能散发毒气，黄帝只得停战。后来黄帝发现，这些妖魔鬼怪原来最怕龙的声音，可是不能每一次都找龙来帮忙啊，于是黄帝便四处寻找类似龙吟的声音，经过不断尝试，他发现原来羚羊的角做的号吹起来的声音最像龙的声音。于是，他连夜制作了50个羚羊角做的号。第二天双方对阵的时候，50个号角一起吹响，声音低沉、回环婉转，像龙吟一样响彻天地之间，魑魅魍魉被吓得魂不附体，一个个心如锤击，肝胆俱裂。黄帝的将领见状，立刻上前去斩杀了这些妖魔；同时，黄帝的士兵势如破竹，一直将蚩尤的军队逼退到黎山之中，蚩尤也最终战死在黎山。

这场战争持续时间很长，经过无数次激烈的战斗，最终以黄帝的大获全胜告终。因为害怕蚩尤死后还会作怪，黄帝便将蚩尤的脑袋砍了下来，将他的身体和头颅分别埋葬在不同的地方，其他部落看到黄帝的威武，纷纷归附，华夏族的领土进一步延伸到长江流域，各地的文化也开始融合，逐渐形成了兼容并包的中华文化。

河南省新密具茨山的云岩宫是传说中黄帝的行宫、寝宫，这一代流传着黄帝与蚩尤的战争传说。据说黄帝败退至此练兵，与大臣风后、力牧研究八卦阵兵法，云岩宫有唐代独孤及的《云岩宫风后八阵图记》

Fengbo wielded his sword, the wind suddenly raged, and the water from Yinglong was blown back, and it swept back into the Yellow Emperor's army. The soldiers were suddenly sprayed by the water, and were forced to withdraw. Chiyou's army took the opportunity to pounce again. Not to be outdone, Yinglong spread his wings, flew high into the sky and sprayed water from his mouth, forming a water column that surrounded Chiyou's troops like a waterfall. But as Yushi just waved his finger, the water column immediately poured down, and soon converged into a river and rushed towards the Yellow Emperor's army. Chiyou soon followed up the victory, and the Yellow Emperor's army was defeated.

Just as the Yellow Emperor wanted to retreat, from the northwest sky came a goddess with pretty feathers. She flew down to the Yellow Emperor and said to him, "Don't hurry to retreat. I can break his formation." Then she took out a fan and waved it at the wind and rain, which suddenly calmed them. She pulled out a feather from her wing and put it on her palm. The feather instantly turned into a stick. It just took a split second for the stick to change from being slender to being thick. The stick then emitted a huge beam of light, shooting at Fengbo and Yushi. Chiyou's soldiers were sweating profusely and unable to walk steadily. The Yellow Emperor's helper was revealed as the Goddess of Drought, who lived on the Kunlun Mountains. She heard that the Yellow Emperor was in trouble and came to assist him.

As Chiyou suffered a defeat, he was on tenterhooks all day long, feeling restless. All at once, he came up with an idea. He asked his soldiers to challenge the enemy, and then pretend to be defeated, so as to entice the Yellow Emperor's army into a valley. His soldiers did as Chiyou asked and he stood outside the valley, holding a large sack in both hands, and casting fog towards the Yellow Emperor's army. The fog was so thick that the Yellow Emperor's army lost their direction. The soldiers were in chaos, trampling on each other, screaming and crying for help. When the sound made by the soldiers completely faded away, Chiyou put away his sacks and the fog dissipated. Corpses lay all over the valley and only a very small number of soldiers survived. The Yellow Emperor's army went through such a catastrophe that he locked himself in his room all day, trying to figure out a countermeasure. One day, a woman with a human head and a bird body landed in front of the Yellow Emperor and said to him, "I am Xuannü from

碑，碑文记载黄帝与风后创制八阵图，可以"星驰天旋，雷动山破"，威力无穷。之后黄帝平定中原，放马南山，葬兵符于云岩宫深涧中，以表今后天下太平。在云岩宫附近还有许多地名传说都与黄帝的活动相关，如养马庄(养马处)、仓王庄(储粮处)、饮马河等。具茨山中也有很多与黄帝相关的传说与遗迹，《庄子》中说黄帝登具茨山求访贤人大隗，《汉书》《淮南子》中也有黄帝拜华盖童子于具茨山的记载。具茨山的风后顶之南有大鸿山，得名于屯兵其上的黄帝的大臣大鸿，山上还有传说中的避暑宫、御花园、擂鼓台等。

颛顼和帝喾

在《山海经》中，颛顼是黄帝的孙子，在黄帝之后继位。颛顼在史书中，是一位政教合一的大巫神，在西汉的《淮南子》中，他是北方天帝，统治着广大而寒冷的北方大地，他下令"绝地天通"，整顿天人秩序，杜绝人神交流之途，使人与神不能再私自来往，维护神的尊严，树立了氏族首领的权威。他还制定出各种礼仪制度来维护社会道德。例如，他规定兄妹不准婚配，规定男女有别，长幼有序，还规定百姓要按时祭祀祖先和天地全神。同时，规定人们在祭祀之前要洁净身心，要真诚地去祭祀，可以说，颛顼进行了一次大规模的制度变革和宗教改革。

传说，颛顼非常喜欢音乐。据说有一天他感到微风缓缓吹来，那风或大或小，或多或少，或紧或慢，发出了悦耳的声音，声音时而如丝竹嘤嘤，时而如钟鼓锵锵。颛顼陶醉在这美妙的声音中，高兴得手舞足蹈，于是命令自己的臣子飞龙效仿风的声音创作了一首叫《承云》的乐曲，颛顼把它献给了祖父黄帝，黄帝听后大加赞赏。

颛顼还对原来的历法进行了变革，第一次将一年定为360天，而且通过观察星辰天象的运行，进一步将四季制定二十四节气，并规定了在每个节气内人们应该做的事情。从此以后，人们能够充分利用四时节令

the heaven. I know you are in a predicament, so I have come to give you this military book." The Yellow Emperor thanked her, and after studying the military book thoroughly, he ordered twelve southward-pointing carts, each of which had a little wooden man with outstretched arms on it. No matter how the carts were running, the hands of the little wooden men always pointed to the direction of the south. When Chiyou cast the fog again, the Yellow Emperor's army rushed out of the thick fog with the aid of the carts.

Chiyou, then, resorted to his last trump card. He sent out a variety of demons and ghosts who could not only make sounds that control people's mind, but also emit poisonous gas. The Yellow Emperor had to call for a truce. Later, the Yellow Emperor found out that what these demons feared the most was the dragon's sound, but he couldn't always ask the dragon for help. Thus, the Yellow Emperor looked around for the sound resembling the dragon's roar. Through numerous trials, he discovered that the bugle made from antelopes' horns sounded most like a dragon's roar. Hence, he made fifty bugles from antelopes' horns overnight. When the two sides confronted each other on the second day, fifty bugles started blaring in chorus. The low and melodic sound, resounding like a dragon's roar between the heaven and the earth, made the demons so frightened that they were entranced with fear as if their hearts were hammered and their internal organs were split. Seeing this, the Yellow Emperor's generals immediately stepped forward to slash at those demons. In the meanwhile, the soldiers of the Yellow Emperor pushed forward from victory to victory without a hitch so that Chiyou's army was forced to retreat into Lishan Mountain, where Chiyou finally died.

The war lasted for quite a long time, and in the wake of countless fierce battles, it eventually concluded with the glorious victory of the Yellow Emperor. Since he worried that Chiyou would still do something evil after his demise, he chopped off Chiyou's head and buried his body and head in separate places. Seeing the Yellow Emperor's mighty power, other tribes submitted to his authority one after another and the territory of the Huaxia tribes extended as far as the Yangtze River Basin. Cultures from all over the country began to merge, gradually forming an inclusive Chinese culture.

In the legends, the Yunyan Palace in Juci Mountain, Xinmi City, Henan Province is a temporary dwelling palace for the Yellow Emperor. The story

种植各种庄稼、养殖各种牲畜，不仅顺应了自然，还大大提高了农业生产力，这本颛顼制定的历法又被称为《颛顼历》，一直被后世沿用。

颛顼的继任者是帝喾。帝喾是颛顼的侄子，兴于商丘，建都于今河南省洛阳市偃师区。他到15岁时，被伯父颛顼召去辅佐，学习参与治理部落的事务，后因辅佐有功，被封到了"辛"这个地方。传说，不久之后辛地水患来袭，帝喾就带领大家把住处的地势抬高，但是加高的速度总是赶不上水涨的速度，帝喾在高台上祭祀，向上天悲愤地呐喊："老天爷，你既然生了人，为什么不管百姓们的死活，天天发大水让百姓活不下去啊？"天天如此，上天终于被感动，派了两位天神下凡，一下子把辛这个地方的地势抬高到水面之上，从此，"辛"又被称作"高辛"，帝喾也就成了高辛氏。颛顼觉得自己的侄子有德有才，勤政爱民，就把位置让给了帝喾，自己则退居山林修养身心了。

帝喾跟伯父颛顼一样，也十分热爱音乐。他即位后，不仅命乐工制作了鼓、钟、磬等乐器，而且编制了舞蹈，这音乐十分动听，连凤凰都能被吸引过来，伴随着音乐翩翩起舞。据说帝喾管理百姓，就像雨水浇灌农田一样不偏不倚，而且自帝喾时起，天下基本稳定，再也不像之前有那么多的战争，所以自帝喾之后的继任者不再担心战争的侵扰，只需要专心致力于国家发展即可。

颛顼和帝喾当政期间，各种动物植物、大神小神，凡是日月照临的地方，没有不归顺的，疆土得到了进一步的开拓。颛顼和帝喾后来也成了人文始祖，受万世敬仰。

河南省内黄县梁庄镇三杨庄村，北靠一个大沙岗，南邻干涸的硝河坡，被一片树林包围的正中间，有一座"二帝陵"，这就是颛顼和帝喾的合陵。颛顼陵居东，帝喾陵居西，两陵相距60米，陵墓四周有围墙。据史书记载，"二帝陵"建筑宏伟，碑碣林立，松柏葱郁，历代帝王祭祀不绝。如今，"二帝陵"已经成了河南省"省级文物保护单位"。关于帝喾和颛顼的传说，也一直在这片土地上流传着。

regarding the war between the Yellow Emperor and Chiyou has been passed down from one generation to another around this region. It is said that the Yellow Emperor once retreated to this place to train his troops and study the Eight Trigrams with his ministers Fenghou and Limu. In the Yunyan Palace, there was a tablet named "the Eight Formations by Fenghou in Yunyan Palace" created by Dugu Ji in the Tang Dynasty (618 AD-907 AD). The tablet recorded how the Yellow Emperor and Fenghou invented the eight formations, which had infinite power to "spin the sky and break the thunder", as is documented on the tablet. Afterwards, the Yellow Emperor pacified the Central Plains and buried the commander's seal in the deep stream of Yunyan Palace, representing that the whole world was at peace ever since. In the vicinity of Yunyan Palace, there are many place names and legends related to the activities of the Yellow Emperor, such as Yangmazhuang Village (horse-raising site), Cangwangzhuang Village (grain storage site), Yinma River (the river from which horses drink water), to name just a few. In Juci Mountain, there are also a wide range of legends and relics with respect to the Yellow Emperor. According to *Zhuangzi*, the Yellow Emperor once went to Juci Mountain to visit Dakui, a sage. It's recorded in *Han Shu* and *Huainanzi* that the Yellow Emperor worshipped the Huagai Tongzi in Juci Mountain. On the south of Fenghou Peak of Juci Mountain is Dahong Mountain, named after Dahong, the minister of the Yellow Emperor who stationed troops on it. There are also the legendary Summer Palace, Imperial Garden and the Drumming Stage on Dahong Mountain.

Zhuanxu and Emperor Ku

In the book of *The Classic of Mountains and Seas*, Zhuanxu was the grandson of the Yellow Emperor and succeeded to the throne after him. Zhuanxu, in history books, was a great wizard who combined politics and religion. According to *Huainanzi* of the Western Han Dynasty (206 BC-25 AD), Zhuanxu was the emperor of the north, ruling over the vast and frigid northern land. His rule was committed to rectify the order between heaven and man, and put an end to the private communication between man and god so as to maintain the dignity of god and establish the authority of the clan leader. He

贤君唐尧

尧，姓伊祁，名放勋，号陶唐氏，史称唐尧。他是继炎帝、黄帝之后，又一个颇有威望的部落首领，也是我国历史上一位非常著名的贤明君主，是后来中国所有皇帝学习的榜样。由于尧节俭勤劳、严于律己，关心人民，所以流传下来了很多关于尧的佳话。

传说，尧的生活非常简朴，住在茅草盖的房子里，屋子里的大梁和柱子，都是用没有经过任何加工的原木做的。他吃的是粗米饭，喝的是野菜汤，衣服也只有两件，一件是冬天穿的兽皮，另一件是夏天披的麻布。平时吃饭也就用泥碗土钵。但尧对百姓非常仁爱，还非常善于发现和使用人才，他手下的名臣很多，像管理司法的皋陶、管理教育的夔、管理农业的弃，都是十分有能力且负责任的人。另外，为了方便管理，他建立了很有效率的行政机构，是中国政治制度的萌芽。

尧办事从来不独断专行，无论大事还是小事，他都会征求大家的意见，同大家商量之后再做决定。尧年老后的一天，一如往常把大家召集起来，商量继承人的问题，大家一致推举尧的儿子丹朱为下一任国君，可是尧对丹朱的品行和能力都不满意。为了给子民找一个合适的继承人，尧遍访天下贤人。起初，他听说嵩山脚下的许由贤德，当他千辛万苦地找到许由的时候，不愿意涉足政治的许由却避而不见；尧又听说历山脚下有一个贤人舜，又急忙跑去拜访他，在对舜进行了一番考察之后，他再次把大家召集起来，说："天下如果交给我的儿子丹朱，百姓就会受到损害，只有丹朱能得到好处；但如果将天下交给舜，那么只有丹朱会受到损害，而百姓都可以得到好处。我不愿意损害天下，独独让我的儿子得利，所以我打算将位置传给舜。"大家没有想到尧能这么大公无私，况且尧说得有道理，便都支持了尧的决定，尧把君主的位置交给了德才兼备的舜，还把自己的两个女儿娥皇和女英都嫁给了舜，这就

also developed various etiquette systems to promote social morality. For instance, Zhuanxu decreed that brothers and sisters were not allowed to marry each other, that a distinction should be made between males and females, and that people should offer sacrifices at appropriate times to their ancestors as well as the gods of heaven and earth. In the meanwhile, it was also stipulated that people should cleanse their body and mind before offering sacrifices, which ought to be sincere and wholehearted. It's safe to say that Zhuanxu carried out a large-scale reform in terms of both institution and religion.

Legend has it that Zhuanxu was very keen on music. It is said that one day he felt a gentle breeze blowing slowly. The breeze varied as intense and gentle, strong and light, swift and slow, and it made a melodious sound, just as musical instruments do. So intoxicated was Zhuanxu with this wonderful sound that he danced with joy. Then, he ordered his courtier Feilong to mimic the sound of the wind to compose a piece of music called "Chengyun". Zhuanxu dedicated it to his grandfather the Yellow Emperor, who heaped praise on it.

Zhuanxu also reformed the original calendar and defined that there were 360 days in a year for the first time. By virtue of the observation on the movements of the stars and celestial phenomena, he further formulated the 24 solar terms for the four seasons and stipulated what people should do during each solar term. From this time forward, people could get the utmost benefit from the four seasons for planting a variety of crops and breeding different types of livestock, which not only conformed to nature, but also greatly improved productivity. The calendar invented by Zhuanxu is known as the "Zhuanxu calendar", and it remained a guide for later generations.

The successor of Zhuanxu was his nephew Emperor Ku. Emperor Ku rose from obscure beginnings in today's Shangqiu City, Henan Province and he established his capital in present-day Yanshi District, Luoyang City, Henan Province. At the age of fifteen, Emperor Ku was summoned by his uncle Zhuanxu to assist him and learn to participate in the administrative affairs of the tribes. Later, he was granted the land of "Xin" as his fiefdom due to his contributions. In the legends about the land of Xin, when Xin was struck by floods, Emperor Ku led his people to raise the land on which they resided, but increasing the height of the land failed to keep up with the speed of the rising waters. Emperor Ku stood

第二章　圣王神话

on a high platform to offer sacrifices to heaven and cried out with indignation, "God, since you have created human beings, why don't you care about their lives instead of inflicting flood water upon them and making them struggle to survive?" Ku practiced the same rite day in and day out. Heaven was eventually moved by him and dispatched two gods to raise the land above the waters. Henceforward, Xin was also called by the name of "Gaoxin", and Emperor Ku had Gaoxin as his surname. (The character "gao" means being high in Chinese.) Zhuanxu concluded that his nephew was virtuous, talented, diligent in government and a lover of the people, so he voluntarily abdicated the throne in favor of Ku and retired to the mountains to cultivate his heart and nature.

Like his uncle Zhuanxu, Emperor Ku also had a passionate interest in music. After he ascended to the throne, he not only ordered the musicians to make drums, bells, chimes and other musical instruments, but also choreographed dances. The music was so beautiful that even the phoenix was attracted and started dancing with it. It is said that Emperor Ku governed the people as impartially as rainwater irrigated the farmland, and since his era, the world had been basically stable, and there were not as many wars as before. Therefore, the successors of Emperor Ku no longer needed to worry about wars, and were able to concentrate on the development of the country.

During the reign of Zhuanxu and Emperor Ku, all types of animals and plants, and all kinds of gods, great or small, wherever the sun and the moon shed light, never refused to pay allegiance to them, and the territory of the Chinese people was further expanded. Zhuanxu and Emperor Ku became the collective ancestors of the Chinese nation and were worshiped through the ages.

In Sanyangzhuang Village, Liangzhuang Township, Neihuang County, Henan Province, in the middle of a grove, there is the Mausoleum of Two Emperors, to the north of which lies a big sand hill and to the south lies the dry Xiao River slope. This is the place where Zhuanxu and Emperor Ku are buried. Zhuanxu's Mausoleum is located in the east and Emperor Ku's Mausoleum lies in the west. The two mausoleums are sixty meters apart and surrounded by walls. According to historical records, the tombs were made as grand architecture, had numerous stone tablets, were surrounded by lush pines and cypresses, and many of the emperors of the past dynasties have continued to offer sacrifices there. Today,

是所谓的"尧舜禅让"。尧在退位后，并没有同时将权力交到舜的手中，而是一边教导舜，一边继续考察舜，直到舜能够完全处理国家事务，他才真正卸下了君主的重任，但即便如此，他仍然继续关注国事，还经常巡视天下，做了许多利国利民的事情。

尧活了100多岁，去世当天，百姓非常悲伤，就好像死去的是自己的亲生父母一样，百姓们自发组织了哀悼活动，并且在三年内都没有人演奏音乐，他们用这样的方式来表达对尧的思念。

直到今天，全国各地还分布着大大小小的尧庙，尧陵就在今山西省临汾城的东北，陵前还有一座祠宇，民间更是口耳相传着有关尧的故事，唐尧传说已经成为几千年来世代相传的中华文化遗产，也成了中华民族鼓励人们贤能向善、仁厚诚信、共享和谐的精神财富！

德王虞舜

舜，姓姚，号有虞氏，名重华，史称虞舜。他的出生就非常传奇，传说舜的父亲叫虞成，母亲叫五英。有一天，五英上山砍柴，刚要下山时，看到一条大彩虹从半空中向她扑来，五英便怀孕了，而且怀孕9年，生下一个会说话的小男孩。这孩子两只眼睛里都有两个瞳仁，夫妻俩就给孩子取名重华。

在舜的神话传说中最为后人称道的是他的德行，而《史记》中记载最详细的也是他孝顺礼让的传说事迹，司马迁对此评价说，天下美好的德行都是从舜开始的。五英在生下舜不久后就去世了，随后虞成又娶一妻，后一任妻子怀孕生下了一个儿子，取名象。后来虞成的眼睛出了问题，双目失明，继母就经常在虞成面前说舜的坏话，慢慢地虞成越来越宠爱后妻和后妻的孩子，对舜越来越不好，只要舜有一点儿过失就严厉惩罚他。舜的继母和弟弟也总是找舜的麻烦。

有一次，家里谷仓的屋顶漏水了，继母就让舜上去修补，等舜爬上

the Mausoleum of Two Emperors has been listed as a provincial cultural heritage site in Henan Province. Legends about Emperor Ku and Zhuanxu have circulated in this land since antiquity.

The Great Emperor Yao

Emperor Yao, whose last name was Yiqi and first name was Fangxun, also had his clan name Taotang and was historically called Tangyao. He was one of the most famous Emperors in the history of China and another respected tribal chief alongside the Yan Emperor and the Yellow Emperor (Huangdi), the three of them being considered the best models for subsequent Emperors. Many enlightening stories about Yao handed down due to his brilliant qualities, such as his industriousness, self-discipline and concern for the people.

Legend has it that Yao had a very simple life, living in a thatched house of which the girders and pillars were made of unprocessed logs. Although he ate coarse rice, drank wild vegetable soup and just had one hide in winter and one sackcloth in summer for clothing, he was still very kind to his people. He was good at identifying talented leaders, such as Gaotao, who was in charge of the administration of justice; Kui, who was in charge of education; and Qi, who was in charge of agriculture. They were all capable and responsible. In addition, in order to facilitate the management of the country, he established an administrative organ with high-efficiency, which was the germination of China's political system.

Yao was very democratic in his approach to ruling because he would consult with everyone before making any decisions. Here is a story about it. When Yao was in his old age, he gathered people around one day in order to decide who could be the heir to the throne. The people unanimously elected Yao's son Danzhu as the next emperor. But Danzhu's poor qualities and abilities made Yao hesitate. Hence, Yao walked out and visited all the wise counselors in order to find one who was able to take care of his people. At first, he found Xuyou who was living at the foot of Songshan Mountain. But Xuyou refused as he didn't want to get involved in politics. Then Yao heard that there was another wise man named Shun living at the foot of Lishan Mountain. Yao hurried off to visit him. After observing for a while, Yao was satisfied to call the people together again and said,

第二章 圣王神话

"If the country is left to my son Danzhu, no one will get benefits except him. But if the country is managed by Shun, everyone will be happy except my son. For me, I do not wish to harm my people, so I intend to give Shun my position." No one could imagine that Yao could be so selfless. But Yao was right. As a consequence, they all supported Yao's decision. Yao gave the position of the monarch to Shun, and married his two daughters Ehuang and Nüying to Shun. This is the story called "Yao Shun Shan Rang". After his abdication, Yao did not hand over power to Shun at once, but continued to watch him while teaching him how to be a capable emperor. It was not until Shun was fully able to handle the affairs of the state that Yao was truly relieved of the responsibilities of the monarch. But even so, he still continued to visit the world and did many things for the benefit of the country and the people, paying attention to the affairs of the state.

Emperor Yao lived to be more than 100 years old. The day he passed away, people were very sad, grieving as though they had lost their own parent. They spontaneously organized mourning activities, and in the first three years after Yao's death, no one played music. They expressed their sense of loss to Yao in this way.

To this day, there are still numerous large and small Yao Temples around the country. The mausoleum of Emperor Yao is located in the northeast of Linfen City of Shanxi Province in east China with a temple in front of it. The legend of Emperor Yao is still passed down and has become a part of the Chinese cultural heritage handed down from generation to generation for thousands of years. It has also become part of the spiritual wealth of the Chinese nation to encourage people to be virtuous, benevolent, honest and harmonious.

The Virtuous Emperor Shun

Emperor Shun, last name Yao, first name Chonghua, was also known as Yushun. There's a legend about his birth. A long time ago, a man named Yucheng married a woman named Wuying. One day, Wuying went up the mountain to cut firewood. Just as she was about to come down the mountain, she saw a big rainbow descending on her from mid-air. Then Wuying became pregnant and remained so for 9 years. She gave birth to a boy who could talk as soon as he was

屋顶的时候，继母却让象悄悄地移走了梯子，并且在谷仓周围燃起了大火，想要活活地烧死舜。火越来越大，舜头上戴着大斗笠从屋顶跳了下来，所幸安全落地，也有传说是火神帮助了他。

继母和弟弟又想一计，他们撺掇着虞成去杀掉舜，虞成犹豫之后还是点头答应了。虞成让舜去院里挖井，井越挖越深，这个时候井口却被自己的父亲堵死了，舜又向旁边挖了一条地道，安全地回到了地面。也有传说是一条大龙穿通井壁，把舜安全带了出去。舜的父亲、继母和弟弟，都以为舜已经死了，正在商量如何划分舜的财产，象更是高兴地拿起舜的琴来弹，庆祝舜的死亡，弹到一半的时候，舜突然出现在屋门口，三个人都吓了一跳。舜看着象手中的琴，问他："你为什么没有经过我的同意就弹我的琴呢？"象还没有从震惊中缓过神儿，只能结结巴巴地回答道："我突然发现……井口被堵住了，以为哥哥已经过世，内心悲伤不已，所以想用弹琴……来寄托我对哥哥的思念。"舜听后笑了笑，没有揭穿他。

父亲心术不正，继母两面三刀，弟弟存心不良，三个人沆瀣一气，都想置舜于死地而后快。反观舜，他对父母仍然十分孝顺，对弟弟非常友善，只要他们有要求，舜都会尽心尽力地把事情办好。日复一日，年复一年，舜的孝德之名慢慢传遍了乡里。之后三个人也不敢再谋害舜了，把舜赶到了今山西的历山脚下去耕田，让他自谋生路。即使如此，舜仍以德报怨，每每遇到荒年，就会拿些粮食接济自己的父母和弟弟。不仅如此，在历山耕田的这段时间，舜不凡的领导才能也很快显现了。他在历山耕作没多久，发现在历山耕作的农民中，有人越过田界，侵占了别人的土地，他就跑去帮他们调解。一年之后，历山上所有的阡陌都整齐了，人们在舜德行的感化下，还纷纷谦让起土地来。后来，历山脚下河滨的渔民们争夺水域，舜又去调解，不久，那些为抢占渔场而打得头破血流的人也争着让起渔场，所有的渔民都懂得了礼让。之后，舜到黄河之滨去做陶器，不出一年，那些习惯粗制滥造的陶工们制作出的陶

born and the boy had two pupils in each eye. So they named him Chonghua.

In the myths and legends of Shun, his virtue is praised by posterity. The legends of his filial piety and comity are detailed in *Shiji* (*Records of the Grand Historian*). Its writer Sima Qian commented on Shun in this way, "All the fine virtues of the world began with Shun." Wuying died soon after giving birth to Shun. Then Yucheng took another wife. The second wife became pregnant soon and gave birth to a son named Xiang. In time, Yucheng lost his eyesight, and his second wife often spoke ill of Shun in front of Yucheng. Gradually Yucheng became more and more fond of his second wife and Xiang, and treated Shun more and more badly. Whenever Shun made any mistakes, Yucheng severely punished him. Shun's stepmother and younger brother also frequently made trouble for Shun.

On one occasion, the roof of the barn was leaking. The stepmother asked Shun to repair it. However, when Shun climbed up the roof, his stepmother let Xiang remove the ladder and start a fire around the barn. They wanted to kill Shun. As the fire grew, Shun jumped down from the roof wearing a big bamboo hat. Fortunately, he landed safely. Legend has it that the God of Fire helped him.

However, the stepmother and Xiang didn't give up. Another new idea came to them. They incited Yucheng to kill Shun. After hesitating for a while, Yucheng agreed. He sent Shun to the courtyard to dig a well. The well got deeper and deeper, and Yucheng blocked the well. Realizing the well was blocked, Shun dug another tunnel to the side and came back safely to the ground. Legend has it that a big Chinese dragon pierced the wall of the well and pulled Shun out safely. His father, stepmother, and younger brother all thought Shun had died. They were discussing how to divide up his property and Xiang began playing Shun's musical instrument to celebrate his death. But suddenly, Shun appeared at the door startling them. Shun looked at his instrument in the hands of Xiang, and asked him, "Why are you playing my instrument without my permission?" Xiang, who had not yet recovered from the shock of seeing his stepbrother alive, could only stammer out a reply, "I found the well was blocked, so I thought you were dead. I am so sad that I want to express my thoughts of you by playing the instrument." After hearing this, Shun sneered with no words.

Shun's father, stepmother and his younger brother were all dishonest,

器精美又耐用。舜把自己在家中尊老爱幼的作风延续到了公共事务管理中，他这一崇高的德行感化了远近的人们，所以凡是舜所在的地方，人们都愿意来投奔他。过了一年，他住的地方便成了村庄；过了两年，形成一个小镇；到第三年，便会变成一座城市。

恰在此时，唐尧正在天下寻访贤人，听说了舜的事迹，觉得他既聪明又有才干，便来到历山亲自考察他。后来，还把自己两个女儿娥皇和女英嫁给舜做妻子，又让舜和他的9个儿子生活在一起，以观察他是否真的有才干。尧还给舜安排了很多工作，舜都完成得很出色，最终尧将王位禅让给了舜。

舜做了君主之后，继续发扬他贤能的作风，勤勤恳恳地工作，让百姓过上了和平、富裕的生活。并且，他对父母孝顺如初，一点都不记旧仇，还派人把父亲、继母和弟弟都接到自己的身边，舜的仁德终于感化了三人，三人也意识到自己之前犯的错误。

舜晚年的时候，不顾年老体衰，还要去南方巡视，结果在途中得了重病，病死在苍梧山。娥皇和女英听到舜病死的噩耗悲痛欲绝，在苍梧山附近的湘水投水殉情，她们死后，就做了湘水女神。

duplicitous and rebellious. They continued to want to kill Shun. But Shun, on the other hand, was still very filial to his parents and very friendly to his younger brother, and would do his best to get things done when they asked for him. Day after day, year after year, Shun's filial piety gradually spread throughout the village so that his three family members did not dare to murder him. They drove Shun to the foot of Lishan Mountain in the present Shanxi Province to work in the fields and left him to fend for himself. Even so, Shun still returned good for evil. Every poor harvest year, he would give his parents and younger brother some food to eat. Furthermore, Shun's extraordinary leadership soon showed itself during the period when he ploughed the fields in the mountains. Not long after he worked in Lishan Mountain, he found that some of the farmers had crossed the field boundary and occupied other people's land, so he went to solve the problem. A year later, all the crisscrossed paths in the mountains were neatly arranged. Under the influence of Shun's virtue, people also gave in to each other in succession. Later, the fishermen of the riverside at the foot of Lishan Mountain fought for the waters, and Shun went to mediate. After a few days, those who had their head beaten bloody for trying to seize the fishing ground also began to be nice. After that, Shun went to the bank of the Yellow River to make pottery. Within a year, the potters, who were used to making things poorly, produced fine and durable pottery. Shun carried forward his style of respecting the old and caring for the young to the public administration, and his lofty virtue influenced people far and near. So wherever Shun was, people were willing to come to him. At the end of a year the small place where he lived became a village. After two years, a small town was formed. By the third year, it became a city.

At this time, Emperor Yao was looking for wise men in the world. When he heard of Shun's deeds, he felt that Shun was wise and capable, so he went to Lishan Mountain to investigate Shun. Afterwards he also married his two daughters, Ehuang and Nüying, to Shun as his wives. He allowed Shun to live with his nine sons to see if he was really capable. Yao also arranged a lot of work for Shun, which was done very well. Finally, Yao gave Shun the throne.

After becoming the emperor, Shun continued to carry forward his sage style, work diligently, and help people to live a rich life of peace. In addition, he remained filial to his parents and dispatched followers to bring them to his side.

大禹治水

尧在位的时候，天下就发过一场大洪水，洪水滔天，大水漫过丘陵，淹没了农田，冲垮了房屋，百姓只能逃到高地或山中的岩洞生活。尧作为部落首领，把大家召集起来并向大家征求意见，想要找到能够治理洪水的人才，大家一致推荐了鲧。尧认为鲧的能力不足，但是大家一再推荐，就派鲧去治理洪水。

鲧便偷了天帝的宝贝来人间治水。天帝的宝贝叫息壤，是一种可以不断生长的神土，而且它遇水会生长得更快，水涌得越高，息壤也就长得越高。只见鲧将息壤放在了一片土地上，息壤立刻化成万里长堤，汹涌澎湃的洪水被挡在长堤之外。人们感激鲧，地面上的呼声越来越高，惊动了天庭的天帝，这时天帝才发现息壤被偷，震怒之下不但将鲧处死在羽山，还收回了息壤，洪水再一次肆虐开来。

奇怪的是，鲧的尸体三年都没有腐烂，不仅如此，他的肚子还越来越大，里面似乎孕育了一个小生命。此时舜已经继位，他听说了这件事情，就派人拿着刀子剖开鲧的尸体，没想到从鲧的肚子里跳出一条虬龙，这条龙变成一个孩子，就是鲧的儿子大禹。禹降生之后，鲧的残骸化作一头黄熊，跳入羽山下面的深渊中，消失不见了。

禹长大之后，得到舜的任命，正式接过父亲治水的接力棒。于是，大禹决定改变父亲的策略，他走遍全国，跋山涉水，总是随身携带各种测量工具，到各处勘察地形，最终确定了以疏通河道为主、建坝堵水为辅的治水方法。

大禹发现洪水最严重的地方在黄河中游，他便带领着百姓从这里开始治理。黄河中游有一座龙门山，横亘在河水中间，挡住了河水的去路，大量的河水流不出去导致水位不断增长，禹勘探地形之后决定将大山凿出一个口子，好让水能够顺畅地流入大海。制定好方案后，禹就

Finally, his three relatives who had given him trouble were moved by Shun's benevolence. They realized their mistakes.

When Emperor Shun was in his old age, regardless of his infirmity, he insisted on making a trip to the south of the state. As a result, he fell seriously ill on the way and died in Cangwu Mountain. The empresses Ehuang and Nüying were so sad that both of them committed suicide by jumping into the Xiangshui River near Cangwu Mountain and thus they became the goddesses of Xiangshui River after their deaths.

Emperor Yu Taming the Flood

In the reign of Emperor Yao, a terrible flood occurred in the world raging heavily. The water flowed over the hills, submerged farmlands, washed away houses, and resulted in great population's displacements, forcing the people to live on the highlands or in caves. As the leader of the tribe, Yao gathered everyone together and asked them for advice about whom to follow. They unanimously recommended Gun, Yu's father. While Yao thought Gun's ability was insufficient, his people recommended Gun again and again. As a result, Yao dispatched Gun to have a try.

Gun stole a treasure called Xirang from Heaven, expecting to use it to control the flood. Xirang was a kind of sacred soil that could keep growing and even could grow faster when it was exposed to water. The higher the water surged, the higher the soil grew. The supernatural soil turned into a dike of thousands of miles as soon as Gun laid it on the ground. The surging flood was blocked. After seeing this, the people were so surprised and cheered so loudly that they shocked Heaven. Then Heaven found out that Xirang had been stolen by Gun, which made him so angry that he not only executed Gun in Yushan Mountain, but also took back his treasure, causing the flood to rage again.

However, things went in an odd way. Gun's body didn't decompose for three years. Not only that, but his belly grew larger and larger, suggesting there seemed to be a small life in it. After hearing about Gun, Emperor Shun asked a subordinate to cut open Gun's corpse. Unexpectedly, a Chinese dragon flew out and transformed into a child who became Gun's son Yu. Then, Gun's remains

和当地的百姓一起凿山。当时的工具还非常原始，大家使用的是简陋的石斧、木头等，工作环境极其艰苦，不仅如此，他们还要忍受严寒酷暑和毒蛇猛兽的侵袭。经过5年的努力，终于将龙门山生生凿出了一道口子，河水瞬间倾泻而下，水声震耳欲聋，黄河逐渐恢复了平静。后人为了纪念禹，也将龙门山称为禹门。

治理好黄河中游之后，禹又将中原地区的9条大河以同样的方法一一引入大海，随后他又治理了300多座名山，3000多条江河支流，不计其数的小河。在治水的同时，大禹还一路上记录了各地的山川走势、土质情况、盛产的物资情况以及各部落应向天子纳贡的等级和物产，并且记载了进贡的具体路线。从此之后，四方的物产都被管理得很好。

他遇到陆地就乘车，遇到洪水的阻拦就乘船，遇到泥泞的沼泽之地就乘橇，翻山越岭时便在鞋底钉上钉子。带领民众治水的大禹，虽然是领导者，可是，他却将大量的钱财都投到了治水工程中。不仅如此，他还总是穿着简朴的衣服，吃着最简单的食物，居住在简陋的屋子里，有时候为了赶路还会睡在泥地中。百姓印象中的大禹总是皮肤黝黑、头发凌乱、衣衫破旧。

经过整整13年的努力，治水工程终于完成了，原来凶猛的洪水被治理得服服帖帖，洪水顺着开拓出来的河道流入大海，也方便了百姓灌溉庄稼。大禹刚开始治水时才新婚不久，他是挥泪告别妻子踏上治水之路的，而在这治水的13年中，大禹三次经过自己的家门口都没有进去。其中有一次，是妻子为大禹刚生下儿子后不久，他经过家门的时候，听到家中传来了儿子稚嫩的啼哭声。"真想去看看孩子，看看妻子啊！"禹心想着，可是他转念又想到了滔天的洪水和受苦的百姓，硬是狠下心来，又一次踏上了治水之路。

因为大禹治水有功，舜就把王位传给了禹。大禹即位之后，再次将天下分为九州，分别是冀州、兖州、青州、徐州、扬州、荆州、豫州、雍州、梁州。同时，他命人用铜铸造了九座大鼎，鼎上分别刻上各州的

turned into a yellow bear and disappeared into the tremendous abyss below Yushan Mountain.

When Yu grew up, he was appointed by Shun to take over the mission of water-control. Therefore, learning from his father's mistakes, Yu decided to use a different strategy. He traveled all over the country, carrying a variety of surveying tools, and exploring the terrain. In the end, the water-control measures were determined, mainly by dredging the river, and then building a dam to block the water.

Yu led the people to harness the flood from the middle reaches of the Yellow River to other flooded areas. There was a Longmen Mountain lying in the middle of the river, blocking the water. A large amount of river water was not flowing out, causing the water level to grow. After exploring the terrain, Yu decided to chisel out a hole in the mountain so that water could flow smoothly into the sea. But the tools at that time were very primitive, such as simple stone axes, wood and so on. The people not only worked in difficult conditions, but also had to brave the bitter cold and scorching heat and the attack of poisonous snakes and wild animals. After 5 years of such efforts, finally, a hole was chiseled out in Longmen Mountain. The river immediately poured down with a deafening sound and the Yellow River gradually restored calm. To commemorate Yu the Great, later generations also called Longmen Mountain "Yumen".

After taming the middle reaches of the Yellow River, Yu redirected the nine major rivers of the Central Plains into the sea in the same way. Then he harnessed more than 300 famous mountains, more than 3,000 tributaries of rivers, and countless small rivers. At the same time, Yu also recorded the conditions of mountains and rivers all over the country, the condition of soil and abundant materials, and the grades and products of tributes that tribes should pay to Heaven, as well as the specific routes. Since then, the property of the country has been well-managed.

Yu, not afraid of difficulties and obstacles, led the people to tame the water. Although he was the leader, he invested a lot of money in water control projects. Moreover, he always wore simple clothes, ate ordinary food, lived in a humble hut, and sometimes slept in the mud. Yu the Great always left an impression on the people of his swarthy skin, untidy hair and shabby clothes.

名山大川以及盛产的奇珍异兽，寓意自己是九州之主。《史记》认为：普天之下，要数禹的功绩最大，他带领人们劈开了九座大山，改良了九片大沼泽，疏通了九条大河，将天下划分为九州。他的儿子叫启，建立了中国历史上第一个王朝——夏。中华民族的历史从此向前迈进了一大步！

After 13 years of effort, the water control project was finally completed. The rampant flooding of the area was tamed, sending the water to flow into the sea along the river channels. It became convenient for people to irrigate crops. About the time Yu began to tame the flood, he got married. He offered a tearful farewell to his wife and set his feet on the road to control the flood. During the 13 years of taming the flood, Yu passed his house three times but did not enter. On one occasion, when his wife gave birth to a son, Yu passed through the house and heard the sound of his infant son's cry. "How I wish I could see my wife and my son!" he said. But then he thought of the flood and the suffering people. He was determined once more to set foot on the road again.

Because of Yu's meritorious deeds in controlling the flood, Shun handed over the throne to him. After Yu ascended the throne, he divided the country into nine states named Jizhou, Yanzhou, Qingzhou, Xuzhou, Yangzhou, Jingzhou, Yuzhou, Yongzhou and Liangzhou. These states represented the earliest layout of ancient China. At the same time, he cast nine large tripods made of copper, on which were carved the famous mountains and rivers of each state as well as rare and exotic animals, implying that he was the Lord of the world. According to *Shiji* (*Records of the Grand Historian*), Yu made the greatest ancient contribution to the country. Moreover, after Yu became the emperor, he broke the original boundaries between the clans, making it possible to create a new administration system. His son, Qi, established the first dynasty in Chinese history called the Xia Dynasty. Since those early days, the history of the Chinese nation has continued to take giant steps forward.

第三章

英雄神话

Chapter 3

Myths of Ancient Heroes

后羿射日

后羿，又叫"夷羿""羿"。他是中国远古时期的神话人物，相传是尧的射师。

传说中，天上的太阳就是会发光发热的三足金乌，最早总共有十只。十只三足金乌每天轮流飞到东海一棵巨大的扶桑树的顶端，为大地和万物带来光明和热量。直到有一天，在尧统治的时期，这十个太阳闹起了矛盾，都想上天遨游，互不相让，一下全飞上了天。天空中便出现了十个太阳，河床晒得裂开口子，地里的庄稼都被烧焦了，山林中因为高温不断燃起火焰。人们只要出门就会被晒得头晕眼花，待在屋里也透不过气，好多人倒在地上再也没有起来。直到晚上十个太阳也不愿意回去，继续炙烤着大地。与此同时，一些凶恶的怪兽也从干涸的湖泊和燃烧的山林中跑了出来，危害人间。根据汉代的《淮南子》记载，这些猛兽有猰貐、凿齿、九婴、大风、封豨、修蛇。猰貐是一种人脸牛身马蹄的怪物，浑身还长着长毛，嚎叫起来像是婴儿的啼哭。无论是见到人还是其他动物，都会连头带脚地吞下。凿齿也是怪兽，它的牙齿的形状像凿子。九婴是一种九头巨蛇，高兴的时候就吐出大水淹没庄田，发起怒来又能喷火，把百姓的房子都烧成了平地。大风是一种凶恶的鸷鸟。封豨是一头大野猪，修蛇是一种残暴的蛇。这些猛兽侵占人们的领地，还残害人们的性命，百姓苦不堪言。

人们实在无法继续忍受这样的生活了，他们聚集起来，一起商讨结束这种生活的对策。突然有人提议道："听说后羿的箭法十分好，一箭能达千里之远，再厚的盾都能被他的箭射穿。"于是人们来到后羿的家里，请求后羿制止这一切，后羿想都没想便答应了下来。天帝知道后，被后羿为民除害的精神感动，送给他一把红色的弓和一袋白色的箭，后羿带着这弓箭便出发了。

Houyi Shooting the Suns

Houyi, also known as Yiyi or Yi, was a mythological figure in ancient China, also known as the chief archer of Yao.

According to legend, the sun in the sky was a three-legged golden crow that could give off light and heat. There were ten suns in the beginning. They took turns flying to the top of a huge tree named Fusang in the Eastern China Sea every day, bringing light and heat to the earth. One day, in the reign of Yao, these ten suns became at odds with each other, and all of them flew in the sky day and night. The river bed cracked, the crops were scorched, and the mountains were on fire. The people couldn't stand the heat; some of them died. At the same time, some ferocious monsters emerged from the dry lakes and burning mountains to terrorize the human world. According to *Huainanzi* of the Han Dynasty, these beasts were Yayu, Zaochi, Jiuying, Dafeng, Fengxi and Xiushe. Yayu was a monster with a human face, a cow's body and horse's hooves, with long fur all over its body, howling like a baby's cry. No matter whether people or animals, it swallowed them all. Zaochi was a monster with teeth shaped like chisels; Jiuying, a serpent with nine heads, could spit out water to flood the farmland when it was happy, and also breathe flames to burn people's houses when it was angry; Dafeng was a fierce bird of prey; Fengxi was a huge wild boar; and Xiushe was a cruel snake. These wild beasts invaded the land and killed people, making the lives of the people miserable.

The people couldn't bear such suffering any longer, so they got together and discussed how to put an end to it. Suddenly someone suggested, "I heard that Houyi is very good at archery and that he is able to shoot an arrow for thousands of miles, and even the thickest shield can be penetrated by his arrow." So people went to Houyi's house and begged him to stop the birds. Houyi agreed immediately. Heaven was touched by Houyi's spirit and gave him a red bow and a bag of white arrows. Houyi set out with no hesitation.

Houyi killed Zaochi, Jiuying, and Dafeng one after another and he spent nine days climbing a high mountain. As he stood on the top of the mountain, ten three-legged golden crows flew in from the east. Houyi pulled up the bow, aiming at the first sun. Houyi's white arrow whistled across the air, straight into the

后羿先是来到了畴华之野,用自己的宝剑与凿齿搏斗,趁着凿齿转身逃跑的时候,后羿一箭射穿了凿齿的心脏。他来到了凶水这个地方,将九婴的九个头一个一个射了下来,又在舜的老师务成子的帮助下在青丘的湖泊中将大风杀掉。随后,后羿花了九天九夜登上了一座高山。当他站在山巅的时候,刚好十只三足金乌又从东边飞来。后羿拉起弓,对准最前面的那只三足金乌放了一箭。白色的箭呼啸着划过空中,直上云霄,射穿了领头那只三足金乌的心脏。领头的三足金乌惨叫一声,便从云端掉落下来,它的身体慢慢变暗变凉,坠入山间的悬崖之中。后羿又从箭袋中拿出三支箭,三箭齐发,三只三足金乌被同时射中。剩余的六只三足金乌慌了,上下乱飞。而后羿不紧不慢地从箭袋又取出一支箭,"嗖"的一声,这支箭冲向天空,一下就将其中的四只三足金乌穿了起来。这四只三足金乌也开始下坠,掉在石头上激起了飞溅的火花。还剩两只,后羿又搭起弓,射下了其中一只。只剩下最后一只了,它连连求饶,发誓以后再也不会乱来,于是后羿便放过了它。解决完天空中十个太阳的问题,后羿来到了洞庭湖用雄黄杀掉了修蛇,在桑树林捉住了封豨。人们又回到了井然有序的状态。

后羿射日为民除害的事情很快就传到了尧那里,尧为了奖赏后羿,将商丘这个地方封给了后羿。后来,后羿又娶了女神嫦娥做了妻子。商丘这个地方的百姓也十分爱戴后羿,称他为"射日的英雄"。

夸父逐日

很久很久以前,在中国北方大荒之地,有一座与天同高的山叫成都载天,山中住着夸父氏一族。根据《山海经》的记载,夸父族是后土的孙子,信的儿子。他们是一个有名的巨人族,有着与其他人相异的庞大身躯,一伸手便能摸到山顶,跑起来一日可行千里。他们因为天生爱打抱不平,曾经在涿鹿之战中帮助蚩尤与蚩尤的死对头黄帝打仗,但最后

sky and shot through the leader bird's heart. It died. Then Houyi took out three arrows from the quiver and killed three suns at once. These actions put the rest of them in a state of panic and they flew up and down wildly. But Houyi took out an arrow leisurely, whoosh, four suns dropped down. Now, there were only two left. Houyi killed one of them. The last one begged for mercy, vowing never to come again. Then, Houyi released it. After solving the problem of the ten suns, Houyi went to Dongting Lake, killed the Xiushe with realgar, and captured Fengxi in a mulberry grove. At last, people were able to return to a quiet and peaceful life again.

Emperor Yao heard about these events and rewarded Houyi, giving him Shangqiu, a place in the Central Plains area. Later, Houyi married the goddess Chang'e. The people of Shangqiu loved Houyi very much and called him "the hero who shot the suns".

Kuafu Chasing the Sun

A long time ago, in the great wilderness of northern China, there was a mountain as high as the sky called Chengduzaitian, on which lived the Kuafu

终于还是抵不过黄帝的手下应龙而战败。

夸父族中有一位族人非常出名，为了方便，我们就称他的姓——夸父。中国古代有本典籍记载了他，这本书叫《列子》。列子是战国前期道家代表人物。全书共载民间故事、寓言、神话传说等一百多则，其中有一章的名字叫《汤问》，《汤问》中写道："夸父真是个自不量力的人啊！竟然想追赶太阳，他追到'隅谷'这个地方的时候，因为太口渴，一口气把黄河、渭河的水全部喝干了。但是他还是觉得非常口渴，准备走到北方的大泽去，但是还没有走到，就渴死在半路上了。他巨大的手杖扔在那里，和他的身体一起，化为了一片方圆数千里的树林，叫'邓林'。"

民间故事说，那个时候天空中有十个太阳，他们不听从天父的安排，每天都想挂在天上，百姓却因此苦不堪言，作物因为干旱而逐渐枯死。百姓不断迁徙，也不断有人因为饥渴倒在半路上。即便是找到了一处新的水源，没过多久这处水源也会因为烈日的暴晒而枯竭。夸父决定要追上太阳，捉住它们，好好教训一番，让它们好好为百姓服务。百姓知道了这件事，他们聚集部落的所有人，花了一天一夜锯掉了一棵巨木送给夸父当手杖。

夸父告别了百姓，便动身向太阳的方向跑去。他一跑起来，大地都在颤动，山峰都在摇晃。眼看着太阳越来越近，仿佛只要跳一下就能将太阳抓在手中的时候，十个太阳便四散逃开，夸父每次都扑空。他已经跑了八万公里，脚步越来越沉重，他感觉就好像有个太阳故意捉弄他，跑到了他肚子里一样，令他口渴难耐。他跑到黄河边，趴在黄河上，喝起黄河的水来。黄河由于常年受旱，水量早已不多，夸父没两口就把黄河的水喝光了。他又跑到渭河边，跪下来喝渭河的水。可夸父实在太渴了，把渭水的水喝完，口渴也没有得到丝毫的缓解。太阳还在头顶暴晒他，仿佛在嘲笑夸父的自不量力。

夸父想到遥远的北方还有一个巨大的湖泊，他抬起脚步向北跑去，

family. According to *The Classic of Mountains and Seas*, members of the Kuafu family were famous for their huge bodies and they were the grandsons of Houtu, the son of Xin. Those giants could touch the top of huge mountains and run thousands of miles in one day. Because they were born to fight, once in the battle of Zhuolu they even helped Chiyou fight with his nemesis the Yellow Emperor. Nevertheless, they were defeated by the Yellow Emperor's subordinate Yinglong, who was super powerful.

One of the Kuafu family was so famous that we simply call him "Kuafu" for convenience. He was mentioned in an ancient Chinese book called *Liezi*. Liezi, the writer, was a representative of Daoism in the early Warring States period. The book contains more than 100 stories, including folk tales, fables, myths and legends. Among these, there is a chapter called Tangwen. In this chapter, we find out that Kuafu was really a man who had bitten off more than he could chew by trying to run after the sun. When he reached Yugu, he was so thirsty that he drank up all the water of the Yellow River and the Weihe River. But he was still thirsty, so he wanted to go to Daze, a place with a big lake, but he died of thirst on the way. His enormous walking stick was thrown down there, and with his body it turned into a forest called Denglin, thousands of miles in circumference.

According to folklore, there were ten suns in the ancient past. They refused to obey Heaven and wanted to stay in the sky every day. However, the people suffered terribly and crops died due to drought. People were constantly on the move, some of whom were dying of hunger and thirst on the way. Even if a new source of water was found, it was soon exhausted by the scorching suns. So Kuafu made his mind to catch up with the suns, asking them to serve the people. The people were all touched because of Kuafu's care for them and they gathered together spending a whole day and a night sawing off a branch from a huge tree for Kuafu to use as a walking stick.

Kuafu said his farewells to the people and began to chase after the suns. As he ran, the earth trembled and the mountains swayed. But on each attempt, he couldn't catch the suns, because they scattered when they saw him, even though he thought he could catch them by jumping. He ran eighty thousand kilometers and could not run any longer. He felt as if one of the suns was making a fool of him and had gone into his stomach, making him thirsty. He ran to the Yellow River

可他越来越觉得每一次抬脚都比上次更加困难，胸腔里的火好像要直接烧穿心脏，让他快要无法动弹。最后夸父用尽最后一丝力气，将百姓送给他的那根手杖扔了出去。"轰隆"一声巨响，夸父倒在了地上。烟尘散去后，人们看到夸父变成了一座大山，而他手杖落地的地方，已然化为一片郁郁葱葱的桃林，树上结满了又大又甜汁水丰盈的桃子。

夸父倒下的这个地方，传说就在现在的河南省灵宝市。夸父倒下后化成的山叫夸父山，在现在灵宝市阳平镇东南灵湖峪和池峪之间。而夸父手杖化成的桃林，就在这山脚下，仍然枝繁叶茂地存在着，所以灵宝市古时候也叫桃林县。而现代的研究表明，在公元前8000年至公元前5000年，中国的黄河流域确实出现过一段时期的温暖干旱气候。一个巨人追赶着太阳奔跑的神话在现在看来或许显得有些自不量力，但在遥远的古代，夸父追日展现了原始人民想要征服自然的愿望。虽然夸父最后失败了，但他勇敢执着、勇于探索的精神却影响着一代又一代的中国人。

阏伯盗火

上文讲了燧人氏教人取火的故事，而因为火在原始社会的重要性，中原神话里保存了很多关于火的传说。现在我们要讲一讲另一位中原神话中保护火种的英雄——阏伯。

帝喾有两个儿子，一个叫阏伯，一个叫实沈。奇怪的是，阏伯和实沈虽然是亲兄弟，可他们一见面就打架，一打架便地动山摇，百姓因此苦不堪言。帝喾知道后十分生气，决定把他们两个远远分开。阏伯被安置在了东边河南商丘一带，做了商星，每天凌晨五点到七点才会出现；而实沈则被安置在西方山西大夏一带，做了参星，每天黄昏五点到七点出现。由此一来，兄弟二人便永远不会见面，也不会打架了。中国唐代著名诗人杜甫有句诗"人生不相见，动如参与商"便是借商星和参星永

and drank the water. Due to the perennial drought, the Yellow River had been running low, leaving only a little water, not enough for Kuafu to drink. He ran to the Weihe River and knelt down to drink the water. But Kuafu was too thirsty. Even if he drank all the water, he could not get the slightest relief. The suns were still exposed overhead to him, as if laughing at Kuafu's over-confident attitude.

At this time, Kuafu had the idea that there was a huge lake in the far north, and he started running toward it. But it was more and more difficult for him because the fire in his chest seemed to burn directly through his heart, leaving him almost unable to move. At last he exhausted all of his strength and threw away the cane that the people had given him. "Boom!" Kuafu heard a loud bang and fell to the ground. When the dust cleared, people saw that Kuafu had become a mountain, and the place where his cane had fallen was a lush peach forest, filled with big and sweet peaches.

It is said that the place where Kuafu fell down is Lingbao City, Henan Province. The mountain that Kuafu turned into is Kuafu Mountain, which is located between Linghu valley and Chi valley in the southeast of Yangping Township of Lingbao City. The peach forest that his cane transformed into is at the foot of Kuafu Mountain, existing still in full blossom. Lingbao City was also called Taolin County in ancient times. Modern research suggests that there was indeed a period of warm, dry weather in China's Yellow River Basin between 8,000 to 5,000 BC. The myth of a giant running after the sun may seem overreaching now, but in the past, it showed primitive people's desire to conquer nature. Although Kuafu finally failed, his brave dedication to the spirit of exploration has influenced Chinese people from generation to generation.

Ebo Stealing Fire

The story of Suirenshi is a tale of the person who taught people to use fire. Because of the importance of fire in primitive society, many legends about fire have been preserved in the Central Plains mythology. Ebo was another hero associated with fire in the myths of the Central Plains.

Emperor Ku, one of ancient China's oriental gods, had two sons, one was

不相见来表达与故友离别的悲伤之情。

而阏伯对于河南商丘人民来说，最大的功劳有二，其中一个便是为这里的人民带来天庭的火种，和西方普罗米修斯的故事比较相似。另外一个是阏伯教会了商丘人民通过观察火星来判断天象，更好地把握农时。现在我们就先来讲一讲阏伯盗取火种的故事。

相传，远古的时候，这里的人没有火种，他们忍受着无尽的黑暗，难以下咽的生肉。阏伯还在天庭的时候，曾被天帝安排管理一方的火种。阏伯在天上看到这一方的人们因为没有火种而受苦，心中十分不忍，他决定要亲自携带一些火种到人间去，亲手交给人们，并告诉他们火种的使用方法。可他偷取火种刚要出发，就被天帝发现了，阏伯便被贬下凡间。阏伯明白，这次被贬是他最后一次将火种传给凡间的机会。他将火种吞进肚子。到了人间，他忍受着被火种灼烧的痛苦将它们分发给人们，并传授他们使用火种的方法。

人们获得了火种，生活质量和寿命都得到了很大的提高。有天晚上，天帝巡视人间，他走到商丘这个地方时，突然看到黑夜中有团团火焰正在燃烧。其中有堆火上架着一头野猪，人们围着火堆欢快地跳舞，还用烧过的木炭在脸上和身上画出各种花纹。天帝怒不可遏，马上发起一场洪水，大水不断上涨，在平地的火种都熄灭了。阏伯十分着急，筑起了一座高台，自己在高台上守护剩下的唯一火种。

洪水发了整整三个月。大水退去后，商丘人民又回到了他们的家园，爬上了高台，却看到早已因为饥饿死去的阏伯和他身下被他死死保护住的火种。

阏伯被悲痛的人们葬在了他守护火种的高台下，而这座高台被他们一直保存下来，命名为"火神台"。火神台至今仍存在于河南省商丘市睢阳区的西南边，商丘地区的人们还在高台上修筑了火神庙，里面供奉着阏伯的塑像。每年农历正月初七火神节，商丘人民都会在火神台上通过放炮等方式来祭祀阏伯，在周围举办庙会，表达对他的感谢！

Ebo and the other was Shishen. Strangely, although Ebo and Shishen were close brothers, they fought every time they met, and the earth shook when they fought, which made the people miserable. Emperor Ku was very angry after knowing this and decided to keep the two of them far apart. Ebo was placed in Shangqiu, Henan Province in the east and became a commercial star (Shang Xing). He didn't appear until 5 a.m. to 7 a.m. every day. Shishen was placed in the Daxia area of Shanxi Province in the west, where he became a reference star (Shen Xing) and appeared from 5 p.m. to 7 p.m. every evening. As a result, the two brothers never meet or fought again. Du Fu, a famous poet of the Tang Dynasty in China, wrote a poem that said, "People are always kept apart, moving like the Shen and Shang stars." This poem expresses the sadness of parting with old friends by referring to the story of Shang Xing and Shen Xing who were parted and would never meet again.

For the people of Shangqiu City, Henan Province, Ebo made two great contributions, one of which was to bring the kindling material of Heaven to the people on earth, which is similar to the story of Prometheus in the West. Another contribution was that Ebo taught the people of Shangqiu City to judge the astronomical phenomena by observing the fire, so as to better grasp the agricultural season. Now let's talk about the story of Ebo's contribution in stealing fire.

According to legend, in ancient times, people on earth did not have fire. They endured endless darkness and ate raw meat that was difficult to swallow. When Ebo was still in Heaven, he was commissioned by the Emperor of Heaven to manage fire on one side. Ebo saw in the sky that the people on this side were suffering because there was no fire, and he could not bear to see their pain. He decided to bring some kindling materials to the world of man himself, hand them to the people, and tell them how to use them. But as soon as he stole the fire and was about to set out, he was discovered by the Emperor of Heaven. Ebo was demoted to the mortal world. He understood that this demotion was his last chance to pass fire from Heaven to the mortal world. He swallowed the fire. On earth, he had to endure the pain of being scorched by fire, but he distributed it to people and taught them how to use it.

After people obtained the kindling material, their quality of life and life

span greatly improved. One night, the Emperor of Heaven inspected the world. When he came to Shangqiu City, he suddenly saw flames burning in the dark night with a boar on the fire. People danced happily around the fire, and painted various patterns on their faces and bodies with burned charcoal. The Emperor of Heaven was so angry that he immediately initiated a flood, which kept rising, and extinguished the fire on the flat ground. Ebo was very anxious and built a high platform on which he guarded the only remaining fire.

The flood lasted for three months. After it receded, the people of Shangqiu returned to their homes and climbed up to the high platform. There they saw that Ebo had died of hunger, but the fire beneath him was protected.

Ebo was buried by the grieving people under the high platform where he guarded the fire. They preserved this place and named it "Huoshentai" (Vulcan Platform). Vulcan Platform still exists in the southwest of Suiyang District of Shangqiu City, Henan Province. People in Shangqiu also built a fire temple on the high platform, which is dedicated to Ebo with a statue to remember him. Every year on the seventh day of the first month of the lunar calendar, people in Shangqiu will sacrifice to Ebo by shooting on the Vulcan Platform, and holding temple fairs to express their gratitude to him.

第四章

自然神话

Chapter 4

Nature Myths

日月神话

太阳和月亮是我们举目可见的天空中最明亮显著的天体，日月的光明、日月的规律运行及其带来的日夜交替带给我们的祖先太多的想象空间。在这世界上，关于日月，几乎每个民族都有各自的神话。中原神话中，太阳、月亮的内容十分丰富。在这里，我们讲一讲太阳女神和月亮女神吧。

《山海经》中说，有两位女神叫羲和、常羲，她们是上古大神帝俊的妻子。在东南海之外，有一个古老的国家叫羲和之国，太阳的母亲羲和统治着那里；另外还有一个国家，是月亮的母亲常羲所统治。羲和生了十个太阳儿子，而常羲生了十二个月亮女儿。

羲和、常羲都是非常慈爱的母亲。羲和很喜欢给十个小太阳洗澡，洗澡的地方在《山海经》中记载是"甘渊"。"甘渊"在黑齿国（一个国民的牙齿都是黑色的国家）的北面，这里的水是甘甜的。也有人说"甘渊"其实叫汤谷，汤就是热水的意思。还有人说太阳洗澡的地方叫咸池，咸池是星星的名字。小太阳们洗澡的地方，旁边有一棵巨大的树，大得顶天立地，树荫能覆盖整个世界，叫扶桑树，这里是小太阳们平时玩耍休息的地方。在现在能看到的石刻砖像上，太阳的形象是三足金乌。羲和给十个太阳都排了班，每一天有一个太阳到扶桑树的顶端值班，为天下送去光明和温暖，其他九个太阳就在树底下休息玩耍。但是有一天，趁着母亲羲和不在，十个淘气的太阳一起到了扶桑树顶，忘记了时间，迟迟没有下来。人间因此遭遇了极大的灾难，后来的故事我们也知道了，天帝派神箭手后羿来射掉了九个太阳。

我们可以想象母亲羲和的悲伤。从此以后，她亲自驾驶着由六条螭龙所拉的天车，带着太阳在天空奔跑。当他们出发的时候，白昼也就开始了。《淮南子》中详细记述了他们行进的路线、地点和对应的时间：

Myths of the Sun and the Moon

The sun and the moon are the brightest and most prominent celestial bodies in the sky we can see. The brightness of the sun and the moon, the alternation of day and night, and the regular operation of their cycles provided our ancestors with much imagination. In this world, almost every nation has its own myths about the sun and the moon. In the myths of the Central Plains, the legends of the sun and the moon are rich in content. Two of these concern the sun goddess and the moon goddess.

According to *Shanhai Jing* (*The Classic of Mountains and Seas*), there are two goddesses named Xihe and Changxi. They are the wives of the ancient great God, Emperor Jun. Outside the southeastern sea, there is an ancient country called the country of Xihe, where Xihe, the mother of the sun, governs. Another country is ruled by Changxi, the mother of the moon. Xihe gave birth to ten sun sons, while Changxi delivered twelve moon daughters.

Xihe and Changxi were both very loving mothers. Xihe liked to bathe the ten little suns in a place known as "Ganyuan" (the sweet abyss) in *Shanhai Jing*. "Ganyuan" is in north of the black tooth country (a country where people's teeth are black). The water there is sweet. Some people also say that "Ganyuan" is actually called Tanggu (the valley of soup), and where "Tang" (the soup) means hot water. Others say that the place where the suns take a shower is called Xianchi, which is also the name of the star. Where the little suns bathe, there is a huge tree next to it, which is so large that its shade can cover the whole world. It is called the Fusang tree, which is the place where the little suns usually play and rest. On the stone carving and brick statues that can be seen now at this place, the image of the sun as a golden crow with three feet can be seen. Xihe arranged shifts for ten suns. Every day, one sun went to the top of the Fusang tree to send light and warmth to the world, while the other nine suns rested and played under the tree. But one day, taking advantage of the absence of Mother Xihe, the ten naughty suns came to the top of Fusang tree together, forgetting the passage of time, they didn't come down for a long time. As a result of this, the mortal world suffered a great disaster. As we know from the later story, the Emperor of Heaven dispatched the divine archer Houyi to shoot out nine suns.

当太阳车掠过扶桑树的树枝时,叫晨明;升到扶桑树顶时,叫朏明……到悲泉时,羲和会停下龙车休息一下,到了"悬车"这个地方,就预示着白天快过完了;到达"虞渊"就是黄昏;最后到了"蒙谷"这个终点站,就是"定昏",天就黑了,这时羲和与太阳就要回家休息,该轮到常羲带着月亮值班了。后来人们又管羲和叫"东母"或者"羲和老母",现在在山东省日照市(这个地名的意思就是中国最东的地方,太阳光照之处)还有羲和老母庙,供奉着太阳女神羲和。

常羲同样喜欢给十二个小月亮洗澡。喜欢给她们洗澡的原因,可能是古人看到太阳、月亮每天光洁如新、光彩照人带来的温馨想象吧!太阳的标志是三足金乌,那么月亮的形象是什么呢?月亮的形象是小蟾蜍。因为月亮总是阴晴圆缺,古人联想月亮拥有着死而复生的神力,而且月亮有着阴性的女性化特质。青蛙、蟾蜍在古人心目中是神秘的、可以死而复生的而且是多产的,所以就和月亮联系了起来。兔子同样也是多繁殖的动物,在神话里不也进入了月亮,成了月亮女神嫦娥的宠物了吗?如果我们再顺着神话的思路进行有趣的联想,蟾蜍不停地一呼一吸,当蟾蜍鼓起肚子变成发光的圆球,月亮就圆了;当蟾蜍瘪下肚子,月亮就成了弯弯的细钩。每个月亮在天上缓缓地完成一次深呼吸,就是一个月时间。十二个月亮排队做一次深呼吸,也就是一年的时间了。

后来,在《尚书》中,羲和成为尧手下一个天文官员的名字,这应该就是神话历史化的痕迹。我们现在看到的汉代南阳画像砖上,还有很多衣袂飘飘的女神举着有三足金乌的太阳、有蟾蜍月亮的浮雕,这些浮雕被称为"羲和主日""常羲主月"。不过,就月亮女神而言,中国人民最为熟悉的不是常羲,而是美丽的嫦娥。

We can imagine the grief of Mother Xihe. Since then, she personally drives the Heavenly chariot pulled by six dragons, running across the sky with the sun. When they set out, the day begins. The text *Huainanzi* describes in detail the route, location and corresponding time of their journey: when the sun passes over the branches of the Fusang tree, it is called Chenming. When the sun rises to the top of the Fusang tree, it is called Feiming... When she comes to Beiquan, Xihe will stop the dragon chariot and have a rest. When she arrives at the "Hanging Car", the daytime is almost over. Reaching "Yuyuan", it is dusk. Finally, when she arrives at the terminal station of "Menggu", that is, "Dinghun", meaning it is dark. At this time, Xihe and the sun go home for a rest while it is Changxi's turn to take the moon on their journey across the sky. Later, people called Xihe "East Mother" or "Old Mother of Xihe". Now in Rizhao City, Shandong Province (this place name means the easternmost place in China, where the sun shines), there is a temple named after Old Mother of Xihe, which people may venerate the sun goddess Xihe.

Changxi also likes to bathe the twelve little moons. The reason why the legends say that she likes to bathe them may be the warm imagination of the ancients who saw the sun and the moon as bright and clean as new every day! The symbol of the sun is three-foot golden crow, so what is the image of the moon? The image of the moon is a little toad. Because the moon always waxes and wanes, the ancients associate the moon with the divine power of rebirth and the moon has the feminine characteristic of Yin. Frogs and toads were mysterious in the eyes of the ancients, capable of resurrection from the dead and they are prolific, so they were associated with the moon. Rabbits are also prolific animals, so in the myth about the moon, they also are said to enter the moon and become the pets of Chang'e, the goddess of the moon. If we follow the mythological idea to make interesting associations, the toad keeps breathing and exhaling. When the toad bulges its stomach and turns into a luminous ball, the moon will be round. When the toad deflates, the moon becomes a curved hook. Each complete passing of the moon slowly completes a deep breath in the sky, which is one month. Twelve moons lined up for a deep breath make a year.

Subsequently, in *Shangshu* (*The Book of Documents*), Xihe became the name of an astronomy official under Yao, which represents the trace of the historicizing

嫦娥奔月

　　学界普遍认为，"嫦娥"这个称呼来源于常羲。嫦娥在中国是最有名的月亮女神，她和一只不停捣药的兔子一起，孤独地居住在月亮的广寒宫中。这座宫殿就像它的名字一样，广大而寒冷。世世代代的中国孩子一边听着故事，一边望着皎洁的月亮，幻想着嫦娥的样子，也为她的孤独感到同情。

　　孩子们都知道，嫦娥是射日英雄后羿的妻子。他们两个人过着幸福美满的生活，后羿想让他们俩永远生活在一起，就长途跋涉，想去昆仑山找西王母求不死药。昆仑山在中原以外极西的地方，是一座通天的神圣之山。在《山海经》里，昆仑山脚下有一层弱水，这个水的浮力特别弱，连一片羽毛都浮不起来，还环绕着一层在不停燃烧的熊熊火山，几座入口都有强大的怪兽把守，一般人根本不可能进入。西王母是昆仑山的主神，在《山海经》里，她是半人半兽的样子，有豹子的牙齿和老虎的尾巴，掌管着上天用来惩罚人类的可怕瘟疫。但是在后来的神话中，她慢慢变成了美丽和蔼的女性样子。后羿克服了重重艰险，进入昆仑山，拜见了西王母。西王母赞赏于他的勇敢和善良，赐给了他不死药。后羿高高兴兴地拿回不死之药，回家交给嫦娥，准备挑选一个吉祥的日子两个人一起吃下成仙。可是，这件事情被后羿手下一个叫逢蒙的人知道了，这个人又贪婪又狠毒。农历八月十五这一天，逢蒙趁后羿不在家，逼着嫦娥交出不死药。嫦娥被逼得走投无路，拿起药塞进嘴里，马上，她觉得自己身体越来越轻，飘飘然飞了起来，朝着月亮飞去，一直飞到月亮上才停下来。等后羿回来知道真相后，只能面对着月亮哭泣。之后每年农历八月十五，后羿都会做嫦娥最喜欢吃的点心，坐在院子里思念自己的妻子。后来，周围的百姓都开始吃这种圆圆的点心，把它叫月饼。

of myth. On the pictorial bricks of Nanyang from the Han Dynasty, there are reliefs of many goddesses with floating clothes holding a three-foot golden sun and the toad-like moon, which are called "The Sun Lord of Xihe" and "The Moon Lord of Changxi". However, as far as the moon goddess is concerned, the Chinese people are most familiar not with Changxi, but with the beautiful goddess Chang'e.

The Goddess Chang'e Flying to the Moon

It's generally believed in academic circles that the name "Chang'e" comes from Changxi. Chang'e is the most famous goddess of the moon in China. The legends say Chang'e lives alone in the moon's Guanghan Palace with a rabbit who continues to pound herbal medicine in a mortar. This palace, like its name, is vast and cold. Generations of Chinese children listen to the story, look at the bright moon, fantasize about Chang'e, and feel sympathy for her loneliness.

The children all know that Chang'e is the wife of Houyi, a hero who shot down nine suns to leave the only remaining one. The two of them live a happy life. In the past, Houyi wanted them to live together forever, so he traveled on a long trek to Kunlun Mountain to find Xiwangmu (the Queen Mother of the West) in order to obtain the medicine of immortality. Kunlun Mountain, located in the Far West outside the Central Plains, is a sacred mountain figuratively said to reach to the sky. In the book of *Shanhai Jing* (*The Classic of the Mountains and Seas*), the text reports that there is a layer of weak water at the foot of Kunlun Mountain. The buoyancy of this water is so weak that a feather can't float on it. The mountain is also surrounded by a layer of flaming volcanoes. In the legend, several entrances are guarded by powerful monsters, making it impossible for ordinary people to enter. The Queen Mother of the West is the main god of Kunlun Mountain. In *The Classic of the Mountains and Seas,* she is described as half-human and half-beast, with leopard teeth and tiger tail, and she is in charge of the terrible plague that heaven uses to punish human beings. But in subsequent myths, she gradually became a beautiful and kind woman. After overcoming repeated difficulties and dangers, Houyi entered Kunlun Mountain and visited the Queen Mother of the West who appreciated his courage and kindness and gave him the elixir of

不过，嫦娥奔月的故事还有另外的版本。汉《淮南子》中记载：羿从西王母那里取得了不死药，嫦娥偷吃后奔月。嫦娥为什么要偷吃呢？有人说，嫦娥怨恨自己的丈夫后羿。后羿和嫦娥本来都是尊贵的天神。因为十个太阳出现在天空的时候人们叫苦连天，天帝（太阳是天帝的儿子）让后羿去教训一下太阳们，没想到后羿义愤填膺，直接射掉了九个太阳。天帝心里暗暗记恨后羿，把他和嫦娥都贬为了凡人。嫦娥天天梦想着回到天界，所以才会让后羿去寻找不死药。也有人说，后羿和美丽的洛水女神又有了感情，不过大部分人认为，和洛神有感情纠葛的后羿和这位后羿只是同名罢了。总之，怀着对丈夫的怨恨，嫦娥偷吃不死药，而且全部吃下，她看着孤寂而寒冷的月亮，决绝地向那里飞去。

你更喜欢哪个故事呢？第一个故事里的嫦娥是柔弱善良的，而第二个故事里的嫦娥是叛逆孤独的。不管她是为了什么奔月，自此之后她都永远留在了月亮上。之后，人们用凡间正常人的生活体验为之设想，认为嫦娥单身寡居于广寒宫中，生活一定是非常孤单、冷清、凄苦的，如唐代李白的诗句"白兔捣药秋复春，嫦娥孤栖与谁邻"。人们又进一步设想，嫦娥一定是充满了怨愁和悔恨吧！描写嫦娥悔恨的诗歌成为中国古典诗歌的一大类型。最有名的是唐代李商隐的《嫦娥》一诗："云母屏风烛影深，长河渐落晓星沉。嫦娥应悔偷灵药，碧海青天夜夜心。"诗人独自坐在屋内，看着美丽的云母屏风上晃动的烛影，再看看天上银河的流转，已是深夜。他又看向皎洁的月亮想：此时的嫦娥会不会像此时的自己一样孤独呢？她每天看着这流转的银河星辰，日日不变，年年如此，她肯定会后悔偷吃灵药，不如当年在人间过平凡而幸福的生活吧！

虽然嫦娥是月亮女神，但她的身影在中国人看来总是孤独而凄凉的。不过，如果从当代的女性视角出发，也可以从这位女神身上看到中原地区的女性祖先除了温柔善良，还有独立勇敢、大胆叛逆的别样性格。再仰望那轮明月的时候，仿佛就能看到一位清冷而坚定的女子，在美丽的宫殿里冷眼看着人间呢。

immortality. Houyi happily brought back the elixir of immortality and handed it to Chang'e. He was ready to choose an auspicious day for the two of them to consume the elixir and transform together into immortals. However, this matter was known by a man named Fengmeng under Houyi, who was greedy and vicious. On the 15th day of the 8th lunar month, Houyi was not at home, but Fengmeng rushed home and tried to force Chang'e to hand over the elixir of immortality. Chang'e was cornered, so she took the medicine and put it into her mouth. Immediately, she felt that her body was getting lighter and lighter. She flew up towards the moon. She didn't stop until she flew to the moon. After Houyi came back and learned the truth, he could only face the moon and cry. After that, Houyi would make Chang'e's favorite snack on the 15th day of the 8th lunar month every year and sit in the yard thinking of his wife. Later, people began to eat this round snack which is called a moon cake.

However, there is another version of the story of Chang'e running to the moon. According to *Huainanzi* collected in the Han Dynasty, "Yi obtained the elixir of immortality from the Queen Mother of the West, and Chang'e secretly drank it and ran away to the moon." Why did Chang'e steal the elixir? Some people say that Chang'e hated her husband Houyi. Houyi and Chang'e were both noble gods. According to the legend, when the ten suns appeared in the sky, people cried bitterly. The Emperor of Heaven (the sun is the son of the Emperor of Heaven) asked Houyi to teach the suns a lesson. Unexpectedly, Houyi was filled with righteous indignation and directly shot out nine suns. So, the Emperor of Heaven secretly hated Houyi and demoted him and Chang'e to mortals. Chang'e dreamed every day of returning to heaven, so she asked Houyi to look for the elixir of immortality. There is another version of the story according to which Houyi and the beautiful goddess of Luoshui had an affair, but most people believe that the person named Houyi who had emotional entanglements with the goddess of Luoshui just had the same name as the husband of Chang'e. But for those who take the story to mean that Houyi had an affair, then it is thought that because of her resentment against her husband, Chang'e stole the elixir of immortality and drank it all. Afterward, out of sadness, she looked at the lonely and cold moon and resolutely flew there.

Which story do you prefer? Chang'e in the first story is feminine and

第四章　自然神话

kind, while Chang'e in the second story is rebellious and lonely. No matter for which reason she ran to the moon, she has remained on the moon forever since arriving there. Later, people imagined the legend by inserting the life experiences of normal people on earth, and presented Chang'e as very lonely, desolate and miserable living alone in the Guanghan Palace. A case in point is the poem of Li Bai about Chang'e written in the Tang Dynasty, "The white rabbit pounds medicine, autumn returns to spring, with nobody Chang'e lives alone." People further assume that Chang'e must be full of sorrow and regret. The poetry describing Chang'e's regret has become a major type of Chinese classical poetry. The most famous poem is *Chang'e* by Li Shangyin of the Tang Dynasty, "Now that a candle-shadow stands on the screen of carven marble/And the River of Heaven slants and the morning stars are low/Are you sorry for having stolen the potion that has set you. Over purple seas and blue skies, to brood through the long nights?" The poet sat alone in the room, looking at the candle shadow shaking on the beautiful mica screen, and then looking at the circulation of the Milky Way in the sky, it was late at night. He looked at the bright moon and thought: Will even Chang'e be as lonely as I am at this time? She looks at the moving stars in the Milky Way unchangeable day by day, year in and year out. She will definitely regret taking the elixir secretly. It's better to live an ordinary and happy life on earth.

Although Chang'e is the goddess of the moon, her figure is always lonely and desolate in the eyes of Chinese people. However, from the perspective of contemporary women, we can also see from the goddess that the female ancestors in the Central Plains, in addition to being gentle and kind, also had other characteristics including independence, courage, boldness and rebelliousness. Looking up at the bright moon again, it seems that you can see a cold and determined woman, looking coldly at the world from the beautiful palace.

黄河神话

黄河是仅次于长江的中国第二长河，全长约5464千米，流域总面积79.5万平方千米，发源于青藏高原的巴颜喀拉山，一路奔腾向前，自西向东分别流经青海、四川、甘肃、宁夏、内蒙古、陕西、山西、河南及山东9个省（自治区），最后流入渤海。为什么以"黄"来称呼这条大河呢？因为这条河每年都会挟带16亿吨泥沙，其中12亿吨流入大海，剩下4亿吨长年留在黄河下游，形成冲积平原，有利于种植。中华民族正是在这块平原上不断生长，创造了中国最早的文明。所以，中国人都亲切地称黄河为母亲河。

中国人常常称呼"黄河母亲"，但是在中原神话里，黄河的河神不是一位慈祥和蔼的女人，而是一位英俊风流的男子。在遥远的中原上古神话中，黄河河神被称为"河伯"。在晋代的《搜神记》里有一种说法，说河伯名叫冯夷，他在渡黄河时淹死了，后来被天帝任命为河伯管理黄河。

河伯在中原神话里是一位十分浪漫多情的男神，有神话说他的妻子是美丽的洛水女神。中国先秦时期伟大诗人屈原的《楚辞》中，曾经有一组礼赞神灵的《九歌》，其中一首就是《河伯》。这首诗描写的就是河伯与情人约会的浪漫场面。河伯和心爱的姑娘一起乘着用荷叶作盖的雄伟水车，前面由四条大龙拉动在天上飞驰，他们一起向西飞到了神话中黄河起源的神山昆仑山，一起登上昆仑之巅眺望滚滚黄河，心绪随着浩荡的黄河飞扬。天色越来越晚，河伯想要邀请姑娘去自己壮丽的水下宫殿做客。河伯提前很久就开始精心地营造这座水神宫殿，它的屋顶像鱼鳞一样熠熠生辉，殿堂上都铸造着金光闪闪的蛟龙，它的墙壁由紫贝砌成，点缀着无数硕大晶莹的珍珠。就在他们准备动身前往宫殿的时候，姑娘因为意想不到的变故必须马上离开。在大白鼋和鲤鱼的护卫下，河伯将姑娘送到河边，他们牵着手深情对望，依依惜别，直到离别

The Myth of the Yellow River

The Yellow River is the second largest river in China, ranking second only to the Yangtze River, with a total length of about 5,464 kilometers and a total drainage area of 795,000 square kilometers. It originates from Bayan Kara Mountain on the Qinghai Tibetan Plateau, and flows from west to east through Qinghai, Sichuan, Gansu, Ningxia, Inner Mongolia, Shaanxi, Shanxi, Henan and Shandong provinces (autonomous regions) respectively, and finally flows into tHebohai Sea. Why is this river named "yellow"? Because this river carries 1.6 billion tons of sediment every year, of which 1.2 billion tons flow into the sea, and the remaining 400 million tons remain in the lower reaches of the Yellow River for years, forming an alluvial plain, which is conducive to planting. It is on this plain that the Chinese nation continues to grow and where the people created China's earliest civilization. Therefore, Chinese people affectionately call the Yellow River "the mother river".

Chinese people often speak of "the mother of the Yellow River", but in the myths of the Central Plains, the river god of the Yellow River is not a kind woman, but a handsome and romantic man. In the ancient myths of the remote Central Plains, the Yellow River God was called "Hebo". In the *Sou Shen Ji (Searching Deities)* of the Jin Dynasty, there is a saying that Hebo's name is Feng Yi, a man who was drowned when crossing the Yellow River. Later, he was appointed by the Emperor of Heaven to be in charge of the Yellow River.

Hebo is a very romantic and amorous male god in the Central Plains myths. There is a myth that his wife is the beautiful goddess of Luoshui. In *Chu Ci (The Songs of Chu)* written by Qu Yuan, a great poet in the Pre-Qin period of China, there was once a group of *Nine Songs* in praise of gods, one of which was *Hebo*. One poem describes the romantic scene of Hebo dating his lover. Hebo and his beloved girl rode on a magnificent water tanker with lotus leaves as a cover. In front of them, they were pulled by four dragons and they galloped across the sky. Together, they flew west to Kunlun Mountain, the sacred mountain where the Yellow River originated in the myth. They climbed to the top of Kunlun Mountain and looked at the rolling Yellow River. Their hearts flowed together along with the mighty Yellow River. It was getting late, and Hebo wanted to invite the girl to

的时刻到来，姑娘挥手道别，向东方远行。诗歌的最后，波浪滔滔而来，迎接河伯返回，护驾的鱼儿也早已等候排列成行，但河伯仍旧痴痴地望着东边的方向而不忍离开。

这是一个让人心伤的爱情故事。不过，在很多其他故事里，河伯有很多心爱的姑娘，而且正如有时候会突然波浪滔天，吞噬一切的黄河一样，河伯有时候也性格暴虐，阴晴不定。但是在重大的事情上，河伯还都能有正确的判断。传说大禹治理黄河时，河伯就悄悄地提供过很多帮助。史书记载，有一次大禹正在黄河边治理河道，突然看到一位人脸、白面、鱼身的精灵浮出水面，精灵自我介绍说"我是黄河的精灵"，并交给大禹一卷黄河的地图，然后马上消失在水波之中。后来，人们都相信这个精灵就是河伯的化身，相传这卷地图对大禹成功治水提供了决定性的帮助。

先秦道家的重要思想家庄子所作的《庄子》一书《秋水》篇里，河伯还是一位非常善于反思的人。秋天到了，山洪汹涌而至，众多大川的水流汇入黄河，河面宽阔，波涛汹涌，两岸和水中沙洲之间连牛马都不能分辨。河伯看着自己的大河而十分骄傲，认为天下一切美好的东西全都聚集在自己这里。河伯顺着水流向东来到了北海边，面朝东边一望，看不见大海的尽头。河伯恍然大悟，找到了海神"若"，仰首慨叹道："俗语说，'听到了很多条道理，便认为天下再没有谁能比得上自己的'，说的就是我这样的人了。我听有人说过'孔丘懂得的东西太少、伯夷的节义太轻的话'，开始我不敢相信；如今我亲眼看到你是这样浩渺博大、无边无际，我要不是因为来到你的门前，真可就危险了，我必定会永远受到修养极高的人的耻笑。"之后海神"若"也向河伯讲了很多人生的道理，看得出来他们交流得十分愉快。

在中国人眼中，黄河是神圣的、高高在上的，但是在神话里，人格化的黄河不是冷酷无情的，也有爱有恨，有喜有乐。他是每年上自皇帝下到百姓都要祭祀的对象，一直护佑着中国风调雨顺、国泰民安！

his magnificent underwater palace. Hebo built his palace over a long period. The roof of this water god palace was shining like fish scales with golden dragons cast on the hall, and its walls were made of purple shells and dotted with countless huge and glittering pearls. Just as the couple was about to leave for the palace, the girl had to leave immediately because of unexpected changes. Under the escort of a big white turtle and carp, Hebo sent the girl to the river. In their farewell, they held hands and looked at each other affectionately, reluctant to say goodbye before the advent of the departure time when the girl waved goodbye and traveled to the east. At the end of the poem, the waves came surging to welcome Hebo's return, and the escorting fish had already waited to line up, but Hebo still looked in the eastern direction where his lover went and couldn't bear to leave.

This is a heartbreaking love story. However, in other stories, Hebo has many beloved girls, and just like the Yellow River, which sometimes suddenly surges and devours everything, Hebo sometimes has a tyrannical character, like uncertain weather. But Hebo can still make correct judgments on major issues. It is said that he quietly provided a lot of help when Dayu harnessed the Yellow River. According to historical records, once when Dayu was regulating the river course of the Yellow River, he suddenly saw an elf with a white human face and fish body emerging from the water. The elf introduced himself and said, "I am the elf of the Yellow River", and he gave Dayu a roll of map of the Yellow River, and then immediately disappeared in the water waves. Later, people believed that the spirit was actually the incarnation of Hebo. According to legend, this map provided decisive help for Dayu's successful flood control.

In tHebook *Zhuangzi,* written by Master Zhuang Zhou, an important thinker of Daoism in the Pre-Qin Dynasty, Hebo is portrayed as a very reflective person in an allegory named *Autumn Water*. In autumn when torrential floods come, many rivers flow into the Yellow River. The river is wide and choppy, and even cattle and horses cannot be distinguished between the two banks and the sandbars in the water. Hebo looked at his mighty river and was very proud, thinking that all the beautiful things in the world were gathered here. Hebo followed the current eastward to the North Sea. Looking eastward, he could not see the end of the sea. Hebo was suddenly enlightened and found the sea god "Ruo", looking up and sighing. Hebo said, "As the saying goes, 'after hearing a

洛河神话

洛河是黄河的重要支流，是中原地区一条有深厚历史底蕴的大河，发源于陕西省渭南市，在河南省巩义市注入黄河。洛阳就是因为处在洛河之北而得名。

在神话中，洛河的水神是一位以惊人的美丽而著称的女神，传说她是伏羲的女儿。她又被称为宓妃，因为她不慎淹死在洛河之中，成为河神。因为美丽，几位男神还为她产生了不小的争夺。屈原的《天问》里记载，洛神是河伯的妻子，而有一位与射日的后羿同名的另一位有穷国国君羿，也看中了她的美貌，和河伯展开了激烈的战斗，河伯还被羿射中一只眼睛。还有传说认为，洛神最初的丈夫是洛河的男神洛伯，河伯打败了洛伯，争夺到了洛神。有人说，洛河汇入黄河的巨大漩涡就象征着他们当时战斗的激烈场面。

在神话里，洛神似乎是身不由己，引起了好几场战争。不过她心中到底真正爱的是谁，却从来无人知晓。把洛神的美丽和多情描写得最好的，是三国时期的著名文学家曹植。他的哥哥曹丕做了皇帝后，对他非常猜忌，他怀着悲伤的心情离开洛阳，回到自己的封地。路上他身心疲惫，在洛河边休息。这时，他突然看到一位绝代佳人孤独地站在高高的山峰之上，他的仆从都没能看到她，所以曹植站了起来，如痴如醉地欣赏她的美貌。曹植用诗意的语言，描述道：

她的身影，翩然若惊飞的鸿雁，婉约若游动的蛟龙。她容光焕发，就像秋日骄阳下盛开的菊花，体态挺拔修长，就如春风中的青松。她时隐时现，就像轻云笼罩着明月，浮动飘忽，就似回环的风吹动着雪花飞舞。远远地望去，她光明纯洁，如朝霞中升起的旭日；近一点观察，她容貌艳丽，如绿波间绽开的荷花。她体态适中，高矮合度，肩窄如削，腰细如束，露出了白皙秀美的颈项。她没有敷粉施脂，发髻高耸入云，

lot of truth, I think there is no one in the world who can match me', it refers to a person like me. I have heard someone say that Kongqiu (Confucius) knows too little and Boyi's integrity is too light. At first, I couldn't believe it, but now I see with my own eyes that you are so vast and boundless. If I hadn't come to your door, I would be in danger and I would be highly ridiculed by cultivated people forever." Later, the sea god "Ruo" also told Hebo a lot of truth about life, and it can be seen that they communicated very happily.

In the eyes of the Chinese people, the Yellow River is sacred and lofty, but in the myth, the personalized Yellow River is not cold and ruthless, but also full of love, hatred, and joy. He is the object of sacrifice from the emperor to the people every year, and has always protected China from bad weather and ensured national peace.

The Myth of the Luohe River

The Luohe River is an important tributary of the Yellow River. Being a large river with deep historical foundations in the Central Plains, it originates in Weinan City, Shaanxi Province and flows into the Yellow River in Gongyi City, Henan Province. The city of Luoyang is so named because it is located in the north of the Luohe River.

In the myths of Henan, the water god of Luohe River is a goddess well-known for her amazing beauty. It is said that she is the daughter of Fuxi. She is also called Mifei, because she was accidentally drowned in the Luohe River and became the god of the river. Because of her beauty, several male gods also fought for her. According to *Tian Wen* (*Heavenly Questions*) written by Qu Yuan, the goddess of Luohe River was the wife of Hebo, and from another poor country there was a monarch called Yi with the same name as Houyi who shot the suns. He also took a fancy to the beauty of the goddess of Luohe River and fought fiercely with Hebo, who was also shot in the eye by Yi. There is also a legend that the original husband of the goddess of Luohe River was Luobo, the male god of Luohe River. Hebo defeated Luobo and won Luo Shen (the goddess of Luohe River). Some people said that the huge vortex of Luohe River flowing into the Yellow River symbolized the fierce scene of their battle at that time.

长眉弯曲细长，红唇鲜润，牙齿洁白，一双深情闪亮的眼睛顾盼生辉，还有两个甜甜的小酒窝。她身披明丽的罗衣，戴着精美的玉佩。头戴金银翡翠首饰，周身缀以闪亮的明珠。

这简直是中国文学里形容女子美丽最令人神往的文字了！曹植继续写道：他马上深深爱上了她，他解下玉佩高高举起，向她发出邀请。女神也举着琼玉向他做出回答。但这个时候，曹植退却了，他心里惶恐而害怕，担忧女神是在玩弄他的感情，于是放下了举着玉佩的手，低下了头。洛神为曹植的表现感到深深的悲伤，只见她身上纯洁的光芒随着她心情的波动开始忽明忽暗，她发出了长吟，这哀伤悠长的声音引来了众神，他们陪伴着她，一起在河畔嬉游。洛神身边有湘水女神，尧的两位女儿，也就是舜的妻子娥皇、女英，还有美丽的两位汉水女神，但是她仍旧显得那么孤独而忧伤。她时而扬起随风飘动的上衣，用长袖蔽光远眺，久久伫立；时而身体轻捷如飞凫，飘忽游移不定。她在水波上行走，罗袜溅起的水沫如同星尘，萦绕在她的身旁闪闪发光。

这时，众神准备离去。风神屏翳收敛了大风，水神川后止息了波涛，河伯冯夷击响了神鼓，女娲发出清泠的歌声。飞腾的文鱼保卫着洛神的车乘，众神随着叮当作响的玉鸾一齐离去。六龙齐头并进，驾着云车从容前行。鲸鲵腾跃在车驾两旁，水禽绕翔护卫。车乘走过北面的沙洲，越过南面的山冈。这时洛神缓缓转头，对曹植说："我只恨人神有别，虽然我们都处在盛年，却无法如愿以偿。如今我们就要永别，虽然我们处在人神两界，但我的心会永远记挂着你，我亲爱的王子。"说完，她举起罗袖掩面而泣，泪水涟涟沾湿了衣襟，然后忽然不知去处，刚才因为众神而亮如白昼的河岸马上陷入了无边的黑暗。曹植不顾一切地爬上高山遥望，又独自驾着小舟逆流而上，最后他一直痴痴地等在河边，希望洛神能再次出现。直到天亮，他身上披满了繁霜，终于明白洛神不会再出现，便依依不舍地继续起程。

这篇《洛神赋》是中国古代文学史的名篇，而东晋"画圣"顾恺

In the myth, Luo Shen seems to involuntarily cause several wars. However, no one knows who she really loves in her heart. Cao Zhi, a famous writer in the Three Kingdoms Period, best described the beauty and amorousness of Luo Shen. After his brother Cao Pi became emperor, he was very suspicious of Cao Zhi who then left Luoyang with a sad mood and returned to his fief. He was physically and mentally exhausted on the way and rested by the Luohe River. At this time, he suddenly saw a peerlessly beautiful lady standing alone on the high mountain. The other servants couldn't see her, so Cao Zhi stood up and enjoyed her beauty ecstatically. Cao Zhi described her in poetic language:

Her figure was as lightly as a startled goose and as graceful as a swimming dragon. Her face was radiant, like chrysanthemums blooming in the autumn sun. Her body was tall and slender, just like pine in the spring breeze. She appeared and disappeared from time to time, like a light cloud shrouding the moon, floating, and just like a looping wind blowing the flying snowflakes. Looking from a distance, she was bright and pure, like the rising sun in the morning glow. A closer observation showed that she was gorgeous, like a lotus blooming among green waves. Her body was moderate, tall and short, with narrow shoulders and waist, revealing a white and beautiful neck. She didn't apply powder and grease, her hair bun was as high as a cloud, her long eyebrows were curved and slender, her red lips were fresh, her teeth were white, her affectionate and shining eyes were shining, and she had two sweet dimples. She wore a bright robe and exquisite jade. Wearing gold, silver and emerald jewelry, her body was decorated with shiny pearls.

This is simply the most fascinating account in Chinese literature to describe the beauty of women. Cao Zhi went on to write that he immediately fell in love with her. He took off his jade pendant and held it high to invite her. The goddess also held Qiongyu (a kind of jade) in response to his invitation. But at this time, Cao Zhi retreated. He was frightened and worried that the goddess was playing with his feelings, so he put down his hand holding the jade pendant and lowered his head. Luo Shen felt deeply sorrowful for Cao Zhi's performance. She saw the pure light on her body beginning to flicker with the fluctuation of her mood. She issued a long chant, a sad and long voice that attracted the gods. They accompanied her and swam along the river. Luo Shen was surrounded by the

之画的《洛神赋图》以类似连环画的长卷形式，展现了洛神和曹植的这一段邂逅。有人说，《洛神赋》中的洛水女神是曹植早年爱上的一个女子，她风华绝代，却很早不幸死去。也有人说，这位洛水女神是曹植心中理想与光明的化身，曹植在他人生失意的时刻，幻想出这样的光明女神给予自己心灵的力量。在中原神话中，也有这样浪漫的爱情故事，这说明中原地区的祖先们对美好爱情的热烈追求，对美丽女神美好爱情生活的期待。

goddesses of the Xiang River, Yao's two daughters, namely Shun's wife Ehuang and Nüying, and two beautiful goddesses from the Han River, but she still looked so lonely and sad. From time to time, she raised her coat floating with the wind, covered the light with long sleeves, and stood for a long time. Sometimes her body was as light as a flying duck, wandering around. She walked on the waves, and the spray from her stockings, like stardust, lingered around her and glittered.

At this time when the gods were ready to leave, Ping Yi, the god of wind, screened the strong wind, and the god of water stopped the waves behind the river. Hebo, Fengyi, struck the divine drum, and Nüwa sent out a clear song. The flying fish guarded Luo Shen's ride, and the gods left with the jingling Yuluan. Six dragons went side by side, driving the cloud carriage calmly forward. The whale salamander leaped on both sides of the carriage, and the waterfowl flew around as a guard. The carriage passed the sandbar in the north and the hill in the south. Just then, Luo Shen slowly turned her head and said to Cao Zhi, "I only hate the difference between human beings and gods. Although we are in our prime, we can't achieve our wishes. Now we are going to say goodbye forever. Although we are in the realm of human beings and gods, my heart will always remember you, my dear prince." With that, she raised her sleeves to cover her face and wept, with tears wetting her skirt, and then suddenly she went missing. The riverbank that was bright as day because of the gods immediately fell into boundless darkness. Cao Zhi recklessly climbed the mountain, looked into the distance, and drove the boat upstream alone. Finally, he waited by the river, hoping that Luo Shen would appear again. At the coming of dawn, he was covered with frost, and finally realized that Luo Shen would not appear again, so he reluctantly continued on his journey.

This *Luo Shen Fu* (*An Ode to the Goddess of Luohe River*) is a famous essay in the history of Chinese literature, and the *Luo Shen Fu Tu* (*Painting on An Ode to the Goddess of Luohe River*) painted by Gu Kaizhi, the "saint of painting" in the Eastern Jin Dynasty, portrays this encounter between Luo Shen and Cao Zhi in the form of a long scroll similar to a comic book. Some people say that the goddess of Luohe River described in *An Ode to the Goddess of Luohe River* was actually a woman Cao Zhi fell in love with in his early years. She was gorgeous, but unfortunately died early. It is also said that the goddess of Luohe River is

098　第四章　自然神话

the embodiment of the ideal and light in Cao Zhi's heart. Cao Zhi imagined the power of such a goddess of light to inspire his heart at a time of disappointment in his life. In the myths of the Central Plains, there are also such romantic love stories, revealing that the ancestors of the Central Plains region were capable of a warm pursuit of beautiful love and a happy life represented by the goddess of beauty.

第五章

神仙神话

Chapter 5

Myths of the Immortals

共工触柱

　　共工是中国远古时期的水神,在不同的典籍中,也有叫他穷奇、康回的。根据我国最早的编年体史书《春秋》《左传》中记载,当初黄帝以云纪官,将共工以水纪,掌管着中国的江湖河泽池沼,相当于西方神话故事中的波塞冬。他是火神祝融的儿子,炎帝的后裔,是共工氏的首领。根据北朝郦道元所著的《水经注》的推断,共工和他的部落住在黄河中游河西的贡山,大概是现在的河南省辉县一带。共工氏是从神农氏大部落中分出来的一支,和神农一样,共工也带领他的部落为中原地区的农业发展做出了重要的贡献。

　　共工有着人类的上半身,却有着蛇一样的下半身。最开始的时候,共工还是一位勤勤恳恳、十分重视农业水利的部落首领。他看到百姓每天要抬着水缸走很远到河边取水,再抬回来灌溉农田,十分费力,于是他带领部落的人在农田边筑起了一个蓄水的池子,并在黄河的堤岸上开一个小口子将水引到这个池子里来。共工发明的这个筑堤蓄水的方法给百姓带来了很大的便利,黄河流域沿岸其他部落也纷纷效仿。

　　早年的时候,黄河洪水泛滥,淹没了共工所在的中游地区。共工带领他的族人将山上的泥土搬运下来,堵在黄河缺口的地方,并将黄河的两岸加高,堵住了泛滥的洪水。人们于是更加崇拜共工,共工也因此变得十分骄纵暴躁,目中无人。可黄河从黄土高原而来,水中挟带的大量泥沙不断随着水流堆积在黄河的河床上,河床越堆越高,终于超过了共工筑起来的河岸,黄河又决堤了。翻涌的黄河水从决堤的地方冲下来,被共工筑起来的河岸出现的缺口也越来越多。带着泥沙的河水淹没了河两岸的庄稼,冲毁了人们的房屋。相传是春秋时期左丘明所撰的一部国别体著作《国语》中记载,此时的共工非常狂妄自大、目中无人,在加高的河堤已经决口的情况下,共工还不断要求加高堤岸,脾气也越发狂

Gonggong Overturning the Pillar

Gonggong, the god of water in ancient China, is also given the names of Qiong Qi and Kang Hui in various ancient codes and records. According to China's earliest chronicles the *Spring and Autumn Annals* and *Zuo's Chronicles*, the Yellow Emperor recorded affairs while dwelling in the clouds, and appointed Gonggong to take charge of all the rivers, lakes, ponds and marshes. Gonggong is equivalent to Poseidon in Western mythology. He is the son of Zhurong, the god of fire, and the descendant of the Yan Emperor as well as the leader of the Gonggong clan. As is recorded in the *Commentary on the Waterways Classic* by Li Daoyuan of the Northern Dynasty (386 AD-581 AD), Gonggong and his tribe lived in Gongshan Mountain, to the west of the middle reaches of the Yellow River, which is roughly located in the present-day Huixian County, Henan Province. The Gonggong clan is a branch of the Shennong clan. Parallel to Shennong, Gonggong also led his tribe to make crucial contributions to the agricultural development of the Central Plains.

Gonggong had a human upper body, but a snake-like lower body. At the very beginning, Gonggong was a diligent and conscientious tribal leader who placed considerable value on agriculture and water conservancy. He saw the toil of his tribesmen, noticing that they had to carry water tanks for a long distance every day to the river and then return with water in them to irrigate the farmland. He led them to build a reservoir beside the farmland and he cut a small opening in the bank of the Yellow River to divert water into the reservoir. Gonggong's building embankments and storing water brought great convenience to the people, so other tribes living along the Yellow River basin also followed suit.

In the early years, the Yellow River flooded and submerged the middle reaches where Gonggong's tribe resided. Gonggong led his tribesmen to remove soil from the mountain, plug it to the places where the river broke through its bank and raise the bank to block the flood. After that, people worshiped Gonggong even more, but he became quite arrogant and irritable. The Yellow River came from the Loess Plateau, and a large amount of silt carried by the currents continued to accumulate on the riverbed. The riverbed was piled up higher and higher, and finally exceeded the banks built by Gonggong. The river burst its banks again. The

暴，不断地挑起部落之间的战争。

共工看到无论是部落首领还是百姓都十分害怕他，愈发得意起来，甚至想要和颛顼争夺部落联盟首领的位置。颛顼披上铠甲打算亲自上阵迎战共工，共工早就失去了民心，四面八方的神仙纷纷赶来支援颛顼。长着虎尾，能操控光芒的泰逢从和山赶来，龙头人身的计蒙裹挟着狂风骤雨从光山赶至，长着两个蜂窝脑袋的骄虫领着众多毒蜂毒蝎从平逢山赶来，双方在黄河边展开了激战。但很快，失去人心的共工便寡不敌众，落荒向西北方向奔逃而去。

根据《淮南子》记载，共工战败后跑到了西北的不周山前。不周山相传是昆仑山最高的山峰，是支撑天的九根柱子之一。此时共工的心里后悔极了，又羞又愤，他怒吼一声，冲向了不周山。只听"轰隆"一声巨响，不周山从中间断裂，山顶的巨石坍塌下来，将共工压在了山下。天空马上向西北方向倾斜下来，日月星辰也从原来的地方向西边滑去，大地也朝东南角塌陷下去。自此，中华大地上形成了西高东低的地势，江河大川于是从西向东注入海中，日月星辰也变成了从东向西运转的规律。

共工的遭遇令百姓唏嘘不已。百姓既奉养共工，又害怕共工，对共工的这种矛盾感情正与中原人民看待不断泛滥的母亲河黄河一样。

surging water rushed down from where the embankment had burst and caused more and more breaches in the banks constructed by Gonggong. The river water, laden with silt, flooded crops along its banks and destroyed people's houses. It's said in the *Discourses of the States,* a book written by Zuo Qiuming during the Spring and Autumn Period (around 770 BC-221 BC), Gonggong acted with hubris at that time. He demanded that the embankment should still be built up even after it had already burst. His temper grew more and more violent, and he constantly stirred up wars between tribes.

Seeing that both the tribal leaders and the common people were quite afraid of him, Gonggong became more complacent and even intended to compete with Zhuanxu for the position of the leader of the tribal alliance. Zhuanxu put on his armor and was ready for a fight against Gonggong in person. Gonggong having long since lost people's support, found that deities and immortals also came from all directions to assist Zhuanxu. Taifeng, with the tail of a tiger and the capacity to control light, came from Heshan Mountain. Jimeng, with a dragon's head and a human body, came from Guangshan Mountain along with wild storm. Jiao Chong, having both of his two heads resemble a beehive, led numerous poisonous bees and scorpions to there from Pingfeng Mountain. The two sides fought fiercely by the Yellow River. Soon, however, Gonggong, with few people supporting him, was outnumbered and fled to the northwest.

According to the records in *Huainanzi*, Gonggong ran northwest to Buzhou Mountain after his defeat. Legend has it that Buzhou Mountain is the highest peak in the Kunlun Mountains and that it is one of the nine pillars supporting the sky. At this moment, Gonggong felt so regretful, ashamed and furious that he roared and rushed towards Buzhou Mountain with rage. With a resounding "bang", Buzhou Mountain cracked from the middle, and the boulder on the top of it collapsed, pressing Gonggong beneath the mountain. As a result, the sky instantly toppled to the northwest, the sun, the moon, as well as the stars, slid westward from where they were before and the earth also tilted toward the southeast corner. Since then, the land of China became high in the west and low in the east, rivers flowed into the sea from the west to the east, and it became a law that the sun, the moon, and the stars began to rotate from east to west.

People had mixed feelings towards what Gonggong had gone through. They

蚕神嫘祖

1981—1987年，郑州市文物考古部门对荥阳青台村仰韶文化遗址进行发掘，出土了一批重要的文物，其中除了麻布麻绳，还有蚕丝制成的布和骨头磨成的针。这表明至少在5000年前，中国的黄河流域就已经掌握了用养蚕和蚕丝纺织布料的技术。此外，在河南巩义双槐树仰韶文化晚期遗址中，还出土了用牙骨雕成的蚕，表明在那个时候，蚕已经成为生产生活的组成部分。

一家之中男人耕田种地，女人养蚕缫丝，这是中国在过去常见的家庭工作。发源于黄河流域男耕女织的小农经济是中国传统的经济模式，这种经济模式孕育了中华民族长期的生产生活方式，也塑造了中华文明的根基，这样的经济模式在中国延续了几千年。养蚕缫丝是古代中国人民最重要的发明之一，丝织品的交易也是中国国内经济和与其他国家贸易往来的重要部分。在历代的礼制建设中，皇帝的籍田礼和皇后的亲蚕礼都是非常重要的一环。中国那时的最高统治者以这样的方式来向农神和蚕神表示敬重，祈祷他们保佑来年风调雨顺，蚕肥丝多。

在中原神话中，更多地认为蚕桑丝绸起源于黄帝的妻子。《史记》中记载：黄帝住在轩辕这个地方，娶了西陵氏的女儿，名字叫嫘祖。嫘祖是黄帝的正妃，生下了玄嚣和昌意两个儿子，子子孙孙世世代代繁衍，便有了天下。轩辕丘在今河南省新郑市，而西陵氏部落大概住在今河南省西平县一带。嫘祖嫁给黄帝后，在中原地区传播了养蚕缫丝的技术。至于嫘祖是如何获得这项技术的，在中原地区流传着这样一个传说。

相传黄帝打败蚩尤后，在黄河边上举办了一场庆功宴。在庆功宴进行到一半的时候，突然天边传来动人的音乐，浮现出了五色的云彩。一位身披马皮的姑娘踏着云彩从天而降，手中捧着几只蚕和两束蚕丝线给

worshiped and also feared him at the same time. Such ambivalent sentiments are just the same as how people living in the Central Plains view the ever-flooding mother river, the Yellow River.

The Goddess of the Silkworm, Leizu

During the years from 1981 to 1987, the Institute of Cultural Relics and Archaeology of Zhengzhou excavated the Yangshao Cultural site in Qingtai Village, Xingyang City and unearthed a number of important cultural relics, including linen, hemp ropes, silk cloths and needles made of bone. This indicates that the crafts of raising silkworms, spinning silk and weaving cloth were mastered in the Yellow River Basin at least 5,000 years ago. In addition, silkworms carved out of tooth bones were also unearthed in the late Yangshao Cultural site in Shuanghuaishu Village, Gongyi City, Henan Province, testifying that silkworms had already become an integral part of production and life at that early date.

In the old days, it was a common household working mode in China that men were responsible for farming and women for sericulture and silk reeling. Originating from the Yellow River Basin, the small-scale peasant economy, under which men farm and women weave, is the traditional Chinese economical model. It fostered the Chinese nation and laid the foundation of the Chinese civilization, and lasted for thousands of years. Sericulture and silk reeling were one of the most significant inventions of the ancient Chinese people. Silk trade played a vital part in both China's domestic economy and its international trade. Ceremonies, like the emperors ploughing land in person and queens worshiping Leizu and feeding silkworms, took a significant place in the ritual system in the past dynasties. In this manner, the supreme rulers of China at that time paid tribute to the gods of agriculture and silkworm, praying that they would bless the coming year with favorable weather and productive silkworms.

In the Central Plains mythology, it is believed that sericulture and silk reeling originated with the wife of the Yellow Emperor. According to *Shiji* (*Records of the Grand Historian*), the Yellow Emperor lived in Xuanyuan Hill and married Leizu, a daughter of the Xiling family. Leizu was the concubine of the Yellow Emperor and gave birth to two sons named Xuanxiao and Changyi, and the two sons raised

了黄帝。这个姑娘就是天上的蚕神。黄帝命人将这两束丝线纺织成了绸缎，这绸缎在阳光的照射下流光溢彩，做成衣服穿在身上光滑又凉爽。从前用兽皮和麻布做成的衣服无论是质感还是样子都与它相差甚远。于是黄帝便将蚕和丝线交给自己的妻子嫘祖，嫘祖向那位神女学习了养蚕和缫丝的技术，并将这些技巧教授给了中原地区的妇女。养蚕缫丝便逐渐成为女性的经济生产活动之一，中原地区男耕女织的劳作模式也渐渐固定下来。

而嫘祖也被中原地区的人们奉为人间的蚕神，后世的皇后在每年的仲春时节，都会带领后宫嫔妃和公侯妻室一起祭祀蚕神，以劝勉天下的妇人勤于养蚕。在嫘祖的故里河南西平，每年的农历三月是嫘祖文化月。在农历三月初六这一天，西平还会举办拜祖大典。用蚕丝织成的丝绸也成为中国独有的特产，自汉代张骞出使西域将丝绸带到那里后，便形成了丝绸之路。中国的丝绸源源不断地运往西方国家，中国也被西亚和欧洲一些国家称为"丝之国"。

their offspring. So the kingdom from this family was formed. Xuanyuan Hill was located in present-day Xinzheng City, Henan Province, and the Xiling tribe lived approximately in the area of present-day Xiping County, Henan Province. After Leizu married the Yellow Emperor, she spread the crafts of raising silkworms and reeling silk in the Central Plains. As for how Leizu acquired this skill, there is a legend circulating around the region explaining her acquisition of this ability.

It's said that after the Yellow Emperor defeated Chiyou, he held a celebration feast on the banks of the Yellow River. In the middle of the feast, there was beautiful music coming from the sky, and five-colored clouds appeared. A girl wearing a horse's skin descended from the heaven on the clouds and sent the silkworms and two bundles of silk thread in her hand to the Yellow Emperor. The girl turned out to be the goddess of silkworms. The Yellow Emperor ordered people to weave these two bundles of silk threads into satin, which was quite shiny and gorgeous under the sunlight. The clothes made from it felt rather sleek and cool. Clothes made up of animal skins and linen could never rival the garments of silk in texture and appearance. The Yellow Emperor, then, gave the silkworm and silk thread to his wife, Leizu, who then acquired the methods of sericulture and silk reeling from the goddess and imparted these skills to women in the Central Plains.

Leizu is also venerated as the goddess of silkworms in the secular world by people in the Central Plains. The queens of later generations would lead the harem concubines and the wives of the princes to offer sacrifices to the goddess of silkworms in the middle of spring annually, in order to encourage all women to raise silkworms. In Xiping County, Zhumadian City, Henan Province, the hometown of Leizu, the third month of the lunar calendar each year is the cultural month of Leizu. On the sixth day of the cultural month of Leizu, there is also an ancestor worship ceremony in Xiping County. Silk has become a unique specialty of China. The Silk Road came into being after Zhang Qian, an envoy in the Han Dynasty (202 BC-220 AD) to the Western Regions, took silk abroad. Silk from China was continuously shipped to western countries, and China was also known as the "Land of Silk" by the west Asian and some European countries.

地祇后土

中国古代人在发誓的时候往往说："皇天在上，后土为证……"皇天就是天帝，后土即后土娘娘，这二者是中国传统信仰中代表天地的神仙。中国人以皇天后土起誓，表明自己立誓时的真诚和如果违反誓言愿意接受天地惩罚的决心。

在远古时期的中国，人们对大地的崇拜比对上天的崇拜要稍晚一些。原始人过着采集渔猎生活的时候，还并未意识到土地的重要性。直到进入原始农业和畜牧业混合的生产方式时，土地才被人们赋予了神的概念。人们注意到土地像女性一样孕育滋养着万物，于是便有了"地母"的观念。地祇后土，讲的就是黄河流域的"地母"形象——后土娘娘。《礼记》中记载后土是共工氏的后裔，相传后土娘娘诞辰为农历正月十八，她掌阴阳，育万物。

因掌管四方土地，所以中国古人将祭祀后土娘娘的仪式称为社。如果将中文的"社"字拆开，就会发现它是由"示"和"土"组成的，"示"的意思是祭祀，"土"为大地，故祭祀大地为"社"。后来"社"由祭祀土神的意思延伸为土神。中国有个词语叫"社稷"，其中"稷"便是周王朝的始祖后稷，被奉为谷神。将社和稷连起来，便用土地和作物这两种国家立身之本来指代国家。

后土是由原始祖先祭祀的土地神演化而来的，后土娘娘形象的诞生和道教有着非常密切的关系。土地神实际上本身并不固定是女性，在刚开始的时候，有些地方的土地神是男性。后来根据道教的乾坤阴阳，认为天乾为阳是为男性，地坤为阴是为女性。根据道教的说法，远古时期天地浑然一体没有分开。当天地将要分开时，其中的气体开始上下翻腾。根据气体的性质，清气升天为阳，浊气下沉为阴，所以道教认为"天阳地阴，天公地母"。于是受道教影响颇深的中原地区在隋代前后

The Goddess of Earth, Houtu

When they made an oath, ancient Chinese people were inclined to say, "Heaven is upon us, and the earth bears witness..." Heaven referred to the God of Heaven, and the earth was used to indicate Houtu Niangniang. These were the two earliest immortals representing heaven and earth in traditional Chinese beliefs. Chinese people swear in this manner to show their sincerity and their determination to accept the punishment of heaven and earth if they violate the oath.

In ancient China, earth worship was a little later in its development than heaven worship. The significance of the fertility of land itself had not occurred to them when primitive men lived a life of gathering food and hunting. It was not until the combination of primitive farming and animal husbandry that the land was endowed with the concept of a god. People came to realize that the earth nurtures and nourishes everything just like a woman does for her children, and hence the concept of "the Mother Earth" became common. The goddess of earth, Houtu, refers to the image of "the Mother Earth" in the Yellow River Basin—Houtu Niangniang. As is recorded in *The Book of Rites*, Houtu is a descendant of the Gonggong clan. According to legend, Houtu Niangniang was born on the eighteenth day of the first lunar month and controlled Yin and Yang and nurtured all things.

As she rules over the land in all directions, ancient Chinese people called the ceremony of offering sacrifices to Houtu Niangniang as "社". If you disassemble the Chinese character "社", you will find that it is composed of "示" and "土". "示" means sacrifice, and "土" indicates the earth, so "社" is the sacrifice to the earth. Later, the connotation of "社" was extended from offering sacrifices to the god of earth to the god of earth himself. There is a Chinese term "社稷", in which "稷" refers to Houji, the ancestor of the Zhou Dynasty and he is also regarded as the god of grain. By combining "社" and "稷" together, the Chinese people use the land and crops, which are the two foundations of the state, to refer to the whole state.

The concept of Houtu is evolved from the concept of the god of earth that the primitive ancestors used to worship. The shaping of the image of Houtu

渐渐将后土娘娘这个女性的土地神形象固定了下来。

后土本是道教的神祇名称，后来成为道教"四御"之一。在道教文化中，最高的尊神是"三清"，即玉清元始天尊、上清灵宝天尊与太清道德天尊，而"四御"指的是辅佐"三清"的四位天界尊神，他们分别是北极紫微大帝、南极长生大帝、勾陈上宫天皇大帝、承天效法后土皇地祇。在百姓眼中，后土娘娘不仅是大地之神，而且是生育之神和农业丰收的保护神。宋朝的时候皇帝敕封她为"承天效法厚德光大后土皇地祇"。在供奉后土娘娘的庙中，人们将她塑造成一个温柔端庄的女性形象。在中国玄幻小说《西游记》中，孙悟空常常用金箍棒从地上敲出一个矮小的老头，唤作"土地爷"，这土地爷管的是一方土地，而后土娘娘掌管着四方地界，地位要远高于土地爷。

中国有着悠久的农耕文明，早在6000多年前，黄河流域就有了农业活动的迹象。农业是整个中国古代时期经济的根基，因此关乎农业生产的地母娘娘十分受人尊敬。无论是皇帝官方的祭祀活动还是民间自发组织的祭拜活动，地母娘娘都在祭坛上占据重要的地位。《尚书》中有"告于皇天后土"，历代皇帝登基、打仗或者取得重大成绩，国家有大事发生时，都要在指定的地点祭祀皇天后土，以告明天地自己的所作所为。每到农时，皇帝也会祭祀后土娘娘保佑这一年的丰收。而在民间，与百姓生息关系更为密切的后土娘娘常常被单独祭祀。在当代的华北民间信仰中，后土娘娘仍然占据着重要位置。沿袭明清时期的传统，华北地区在春节到元宵节间会举办社火，也就是庙会，来供奉、纪念后土娘娘，感谢她在过去的一年为农民带来丰收，祈祷她保佑新的一年风调雨顺！

Niangniang has a very close relationship with Daoism. Actually, the god of earth was not invariably a female character. At first, there were some regions where the gods of earth were male in gender. However, according to the Taoism traditions about heaven and earth as well as Yin and Yang, heaven is Yang and male, while the earth is Yin and female. Daoism has a belief that the heaven and earth was a blurred entity in ancient times. When the earth was about to separate, the gases in it began to churn up and down. Since the gases differ in nature, the clear gases rose to the sky as Yang and the turbid gases sank as Yin. Thus, Daoism deems that heaven is Yang and male, while the earth is Yin and female. The image of the goddess of earth was deeply influenced by Daoism. Houtu Niangniang gradually gained wide popularity in the Central Plains region around the Sui Dynasty (581 AD-618 AD).

At first, Houtu was the name of a Taoist goddess, but later it referred to one of the "Four Yus" in Daoism. The most powerful and respected gods in Daoism are the "Three Qings", namely Yuqing Yuanshi Tianzun, Shangqing Lingbao Tianzun and Taiqing Daode Tianzun. The "Four Yus" are the four deities who assist the "Three Qings": Beiji Ziwei Dadi, Nanji Changsheng Dadi, Gouchen Shanggong Tianhuang Dadi and Chengtian Xiaofa Houtu Huangdiqi. From the perspective of ordinary people, Houtu Niangniang is not only the goddess of earth, but also the goddess of fertility and the protector of agricultural harvests. During the Song Dynasty (960 AD-1279 AD), the emperor conferred upon her the title "Chengtian Xiaofa Houde Guangda Houtu Huangdiqi". In temples where Houtu Niangniang is enshrined, she is portrayed as a gentle and dignified female. In the Chinese fantasy novel *Journey to the West*, the Monkey King often uses a golden cudgel to knock on the ground so as to summon a little old man, called the god of land, who just takes charge of a limited area, while Houtu Niangniang is responsible for the land of all directions. Therefore, her status is much higher than the god of land.

China has a long history of farming, with evidence of agricultural activity in the Yellow River Basin as early as 6,000 years ago. Agriculture was the foundation of the economy in ancient China, so the goddess of earth, who was concerned with agricultural production, was highly respected by the people. Regardless of the official sacrificial activities organized by the emperor or the sacrificial

玄女和素女

　　玄女和素女用通俗的话来说，就是黑女神和白女神。玄女也叫九天玄女，民间往往称她为玄女娘娘或九天玄女娘娘。在中国古代一本考证事物起源的著作《广博物志》中，说玄女是王母娘娘的弟子。在中国古代传统的文化观念中，"九"是一个非常神秘的数字。中国道教阴阳五行认为，奇数为阳，偶数为阴，九是最大的阳数，也是最大的天数，象征着高不可及的神话空间。玄女以九天玄女为名，表明了她至高的地位和无边的能力。而玄女的"玄"来自天的颜色，《易》一书有"天玄而地黄"的说法。九天玄女主管战争和兵杀，精通天地之道、阴阳之略。上文讲过，玄女为黄帝与蚩尤的战争胜利起了关键作用，在黄帝打仗连连败退的时期，上天派遣玄女到黄帝面前，教授黄帝打仗的技巧，并留给黄帝一本兵书。相传玄女传授给黄帝的兵法运用起来可以万战万胜，万隐万匿。黄帝便是依靠着这些兵法和兵书打败了蚩尤，结束了这场战争。黄帝十分感激玄女，尊她为帝师，于是玄女便以"女武神"的形象在民间被供奉崇拜。

　　到了六朝时期，九天玄女这个人物逐渐被道教接纳吸收。受道教羽化、升天观念的影响，玄女呈现了人首鸟身的形象特点。在道教传说中，认为玄女是由天地之精神、阴阳之灵气凝化而成的。她还擅长变身，变化成为各种人或物。玄女无事不通无事不晓，是地位比较高的女仙、战神和术数神。虽然九天玄女本体是人首鸟身，但她往往以雍容沉着而又充满智慧的仙女形象出现，手持长剑、八卦盘、照妖镜一类的兵器降伏妖魔。在历代的传说中，曾有很多历史人物得到过九天玄女这位女武神的帮助。除了帮助黄帝打败蚩尤，还帮助越王打败昏庸无道的吴王，将奇门遁甲之术传授给诸葛亮，帮助薛仁贵平服东辽，传授宋江兵法，等等。六朝以后，中原地区供奉的战神由于种种原因恢复成了庄严

activities organized by the people spontaneously, the goddess of earth occupied an important position on the altar. In *The Book of History*, there is a ritual called "to report to heaven and Houtu". When emperors ascended to the throne, fought wars or made great achievements, or there were important events in the country, the emperors would offer sacrifices to heaven and Houtu at designated places to tell them what they had done. During farming seasons, emperors would also invoke Houtu Niangniang to bless the harvest of the year. As Houtu Niangniang had a close relationship with all aspects of ordinary people's life, people held sacrificial activities for her exclusively. In contemporary North China, Houtu Niangniang still carries weigh. In accordance with the tradition of the Ming (1368 AD-1644 AD) and Qing (1636 AD -1912 AD) dynasties , Shehuo, or temple fairs, were held between the Spring Festival and the Lantern Festival in North China to worship and commemorate the goddess of earth, showing thanks to her for having brought farmers a good harvest in the past year and praying for favorable weather for the following new year.

Xuannü and Sunü

Xuannü and Sunü are the black goddess and the white goddess in popular terms. Xuannü is also called Jiutian Xuannü, and people often call her Xuannü Niangniang or Jiutian Xuannü Niangniang. In an ancient Chinese work studying the origin of different things, *Guang Bo Wu Zhi* by Dong Sizhang in the Ming Dynasty (1368 AD -1644 AD), it is said that Xuannü was a disciple of the Queen Mother. In ancient times, "nine" was a very mysterious number in traditional Chinese culture. According to the Chinese Taoism theories about Yin and Yang and the five elements, odd numbers are Yang, even numbers are Yin, and nine is the largest number of Yang and also the largest number in heaven, symbolizing the unreachable mythological world. Xuannü takes the name of Jiutian Xuannü, which shows her supreme status and boundless capabilities. The Chinese character "Xuan" in Xuannü refers to the color of the sky, and *The Book of Changes* has the saying that "the sky is black and the earth is yellow". Jiutian Xuannü takes charge of war and military strategies and tactics, and has a good command of the nature of heaven and earth as well as the strategy of Yin and Yang. As is mentioned

凶狠的男神。玄女作为女武神的形象，更多地保留在了庙堂祭祀、民间传说和文学作品中。

而关于素女，有人说她是黄帝的老师，也有人说她是九天玄女的妹妹。素女对音乐十分精通，相传她是中国第一位琴瑟女乐师。琴瑟传说是由伏羲发明出来的，琴有五十根琴弦。一次，黄帝命素女用这把琴演奏，素女试着弹奏了一下，发现这五十弦的琴弹起来声音过于悲伤，于是她便将这五十弦的琴破成二十五弦，演奏给黄帝听。二十五弦的琴声弹起来好像雪化成的清泉流过山间的石头的声音，玲珑清脆，悦耳动听。黄帝听到如此绝妙的音乐，不禁想起死去的后稷。后稷是帝喾和姜嫄的儿子，是掌管农业的神仙，也是周王朝的始祖，生前最喜欢听素女弹琴，于是黄帝便令素女到后稷埋葬的地方演奏音乐。也许是后稷因此显灵，从此中原大地风调雨顺，年年丰收！

above, Xuannü played a crucial role in the victory of the war between the Yellow Emperor and Chiyou. When the Yellow Emperor suffered a series of defeats and had to retreat, the God of Heaven sent Xuannü to teach the Yellow Emperor the tactics of fighting and leave him a military book. It is said that the military strategies taught by Xuannü to the Yellow Emperor made him invincible. The Yellow Emperor defeated Chiyou and terminated the war by virtue of these tactics and the military book. The Yellow Emperor showed great gratitude to Xuannü and honored her as his master. Hence, Xuannü was worshiped by ordinary people as the goddess of war.

It was not until the Six Dynasties period (222 AD-589 AD) that the figure of Jiutian Xuannü was gradually accepted and absorbed by Daoism. Influenced by the Taoist idea of ascension, Xuannü took on the image of having a human head and a bird body. In Taoist legends, Xuannü is believed to be the spirit of heaven and earth and the essence of Yin and Yang. She is also adept at transforming herself into a variety of people and items. Xuannü is conversant with everything. She is a high-ranking female immortal, the goddess of war and the goddess of divination. Although Jiutian Xuannü has a human head and a bird body, she often appears in the image of a graceful and resourceful immortal with composure, holding a long sword, an eight-trigram plate and a demon-detector. In the legends of the past dynasties, there were many historical figures who received the assistance of Jiutian Xuannü. In addition to helping the Yellow Emperor to defeat Chiyou, she also aided the King of Yue in combating the muddleheaded and ferocious King of Wu, taught Zhuge Liang the art of Qimen Dunjia, assisted Xue Rengui in the conquest of the Eastern Liao, and imparted military tactics to Song Jiang, to name just a few. After the Wei and Jin dynasties (220 AD-420 AD), the god of war enshrined in the Central Plains was restored to a solemn and fierce male god due to multiple reasons. The image of Xuannü as the goddess of war is more preserved in temple worship, folklore and literary works.

As for Sunü, some people say that she is the teacher of the Yellow Emperor, and there are also people who believe she is Jiutian Xuannü's younger sister. Sunü has high proficiency in music. Legend has it that she was the first female Qin-se (Chinese zither) musician in China. It's said that Qin-se was invented by Fuxi and originally had fifty strings. Once, the Yellow Emperor made Sunü play the

第五章 神仙神话

Qin for him. Sunü tried it, but she found that the 50-string zither sounded rather maudlin, so she broke it and created a new one with 25 strings and then played it for the Yellow Emperor. The sound of the twenty-five-string Qin resembled the melody of a spring of melting snow flowing over rocks in the mountains. As the Yellow Emperor heard such beautiful music, he couldn't help thinking of the dead Houji, who was the son of Emperor Ku and Jiangyuan, a god in charge of agriculture, and the ancestor of the Zhou Dynasty (1046 BC-256 BC). He relished listening to Sunü playing the Qin during his lifetime, so the Yellow Emperor let Sunü play music at the place where Houji was buried. Perhaps it was because Houji was pleased by it that the Central Plains was blessed with favorable weather and good harvests year after year.

第六章

灵怪神话

Chapter 6

Myths of the Spirits and Monsters

龙的神话

因为翻译的原因，中国的龙和西方的龙虽然称呼一样，却是两种完全不同的动物。中国的龙是中华民族的图腾，它温柔而强大，降下雨露守护着每个人，在中国人心目中，龙代表着威严、吉祥、活力和勇敢。在河南濮阳，有一个令人惊喜的考古发现，近7000年前的仰韶文化初期，也就是传说中的五帝时期，在一处墓中，墓主人的身边，有一幅精巧的蚌壳摆塑龙虎图，它证明了中原地区的子孙对于龙的早期崇拜。也有学者认为，龙在东、虎在西的布局，对应着春分、秋分时的天象，指代着东方苍龙星座和西方白虎星座，反映了当时发达的天文学水平。传说，伏羲、黄帝都以龙为图腾，这是中华民族的标志，所以中国人也自称"龙的传人"。

在中国的神话传说中，龙是鳞虫之长、万兽之王，它的身体像蛇一样细长，全身布满了鳞片，头长得像马，还有两条长长的胡须，头上有鹿角，四条布满健硕肌肉的腿上长着鹰爪，尾巴和鱼的尾巴很相似。它没有翅膀，却能够在天空中飞翔。它既可以生活在云里，也能生活在水中，但大多数时候是生活在海里的。除此，在小一点的湖泊、河流、深渊中也会有龙的存在。它富于变化，能大能小、能长能短，还能化成人形，它帮助过黄帝战胜蚩尤，也协助过大禹治理洪水，为人类带来了千千万万的福祉。

进入文明时代之后，由于龙能呼风唤雨，便主管行云和布雨，成了风和雨的主宰。在后来的小说中，所有的山河湖泊，乃至小小的井里都有龙王。例如，在小说《西游记》中，东海的青龙王敖广、南海的红龙王敖钦、西海的白龙王敖闰和北海的黑龙王敖顺，作为四方的龙王，分别管理着自己的区域，各司其职，逢旱施雨，遇涝放晴，保护着一方百姓的平安。

The Myth of the Chinese Dragon

It is a problem of translation that the Chinese dragon and the Western dragon share the same name though they are totally different creatures. The Chinese dragon is the totem of the Chinese nation. Being gentle and powerful, it controls the rain and safeguards the well-being of all humans. From the Chinese people's perspective, the dragon is a symbol of majesty, auspiciousness, vitality and bravery. In Puyang City, Henan Province, there is an astonishing archaeological discovery which can be traced back to the Yangshao Culture period nearly 7,000 years ago, also known as the period of the legendary Five Emperors. It was discovered that beside the owner buried in his tomb, there was an exquisite craftwork made by clam shells in the shapes of a dragon and a tiger. This artifact proves the existence of early dragon worship by Chinese descendants in the Central Plains. Some scholars suppose that the layout of the dragon in the east and the tiger in the west corresponds to the celestial phenomena at spring and autumn equinoxes when the constellation of the Black Dragon is in the east and the constellation of the White Tiger is in the west, thus reflecting the advanced level of astronomy at that time. According to legend, Fuxi and the Yellow Emperor both regarded the dragon as a totem. It is the symbol of the Chinese nation and hence the Chinese also call themselves "the descendants of the dragon".

In Chinese mythology, the dragon is the leader of scaly animals and the king of all beasts. It has a snake's slender body, covered with scales, a head like a horse, two long whiskers, antlers on its head, eagle claws on its four muscular legs, and a tail similar to that of a fish. Though the dragon has no wings, it is capable of flying high in the sky. It can dwell either in clouds or in water, but mostly in the sea. Moreover, the dragon can also be found in smaller lakes, rivers and abysses. It is greatly changeable in forms, can be big or small, long or short, and can change into a human shape. The dragon aided the Yellow Emperor to defeat Chiyou and assisted Dayu in flood control, bringing enormous welfare to mankind.

After entering the age of civilization, the legends say that the dragon governs the clouds and rain, and becomes the master of wind and rain by virtue of its ability to control them. Later, the Dragon Kings as fictional figures were said to exist in all the mountains, lakes and even wells. A case in point is that, in the novel

河南民间有个有趣的故事：唐朝的武则天当了皇帝，改国号为周，成了中国历史上第一位女皇。天帝知道这件事之后非常生气，他大发雷霆，觉得不能让一个女人统治人间，于是他命令四海龙王三年内不能为人间降雨。没有了水，田中干旱，一点粮食都种不出来，人们很快就饿得不成样子了。掌管天河的玉龙看不下去了，它偷偷喝饱天河里的水，一个喷嚏，为人间下了很多雨，拯救了不少人。天帝因此震怒，将玉龙压在大山之下，并下了一道口谕：如果玉龙想再回到天庭，除非金豆开花。可是金豆怎么可能开出花来呢？百姓为了感念玉龙的恩德，拼命地想办法，最后，在农历二月初二这天，他们拿出金黄色的玉米和黄豆，在锅中翻炒，从天上看就像是金豆开花一样。于是，天帝收回了旨意，让玉龙重返天庭。从此之后，每年的农历二月初二就成了"龙抬头"的日子。在这一天，河南地区的人们会通过炒玉米和黄豆的方式祭拜玉龙。

在中国的封建时期，龙不仅被奉为执行上天命令的神兽，还是帝王的象征，只有帝王的衣服和其个人用品才能使用龙的图案来装饰。在今北京紫禁城的皇宫中，有一条长达16.57米的汉白玉雕龙，还有一块九龙壁，代表着天子的威仪。在民间，龙因被看作吉祥、喜庆之物无处不在，带有"龙"字的地名数以千计，含有"龙"字的江河也有40多条，端午节大江南北都在划龙舟，元宵节九州百姓都要赏龙灯，还有春节时大街小巷的舞龙表演以及各地络绎不绝的人群祭拜于龙王庙，等等。这些说明龙已经刻进了中国人的骨子里。

据专家研究，中国先民对龙的崇拜与农业生产有着密切的关系。在原始社会，农业收成的好坏与水有着直接的关系，为了能够风调雨顺、农业丰收，先民们创造了掌管下雨的神——龙。慢慢地，龙逐渐演变成了中华儿女的精神寄托，成了中华民族的文化信仰，中国人不论在世界的哪个地方，只要一提到龙与龙文化，就能产生共鸣。龙的威严、龙的神通、龙的正义，体现了中华民族自尊、自信、自强不息的精神。

Journey to the West, the Dragon Kings rule all directions. They are Aoguang, the Green Dragon King of the Eastern Sea; Aoqin, the Red Dragon King of the Southern Sea; Aorun, the White Dragon King of the Western Sea; and Aoshun, the Black Dragon King of the Northern Sea. These kings rule over different regions respectively and perform their own duties. They bring rain in times of drought and stop it when there is flood so as to guarantee people's security.

There exists an interesting folktale in Henan Province. As Wu Zetian became the ruler of the country during the Tang Dynasty (618 AD-907 AD) and changed the name of the state into Zhou, she made herself the first empress ever in the Chinese history. When the Emperor of Heaven found out about this, he was quite furious and considered that a woman was not qualified to govern the world. So he decreed that the Dragon Kings of the four seas should not bring rain to the world for three years as a punishment. Without water, the fields turned arid, no crops could be grown, and famine soon struck the world. The Jade Dragon, who was in charge of the river in heaven, couldn't stand by and see people undergo all the sufferings any longer. He, then, secretly drank the water in the river, sneezed, and brought abundant rain to the world, rescuing the lives of a great many people. The Emperor of Heaven was so enraged that he confined the Jade Dragon beneath a mountain and issued a decree that he could never return to heaven unless golden beans were to bloom. But how can golden beans bloom? In order to show their gratitude to the Jade Dragon's benevolence, the people desperately tried to figure out a solution. Finally, on the second day of the second lunar month, they took out golden corn and soybeans and fried them in the pot, making them exactly look like golden beans blooming from the angle of the heaven. Therefore, the Emperor of Heaven withdrew his decree and let the Jade Dragon return back to heaven. Since that time, the second day of the second lunar month is called "the day when the dragon raises its head", on which people in Henan will worship the Jade Dragon by frying corn and soybeans.

In the feudal period of China, the dragon was not only worshiped as a divine beast to carry out the orders of god, but also as a symbol of the emperor. Only the emperors' clothes and personal items could be decorated with dragon patterns. In the imperial palace of the Forbidden City in Beijing today, there are a 16.57-meter-long white marble dragon screen and a nine-dragon screen,

凤的神话

凤是中国古代神话传说中的一种神鸟，和西方的凤凰鸟还不一样。它生长于东方的君子之国，翱翔于四海之外，只有天下太平、政治清明、国家昌盛的时候，它才会降临人世。所以在大禹治水成功后，就有凤凰在天空中飞翔盘旋；而孔子也曾抱怨凤鸟没有在他生活的时代出现，认为自己没有生活在一个好的时代。

据《山海经》说，凤凰生长在丹穴之山，有点像公鸡，身上有五彩的斑纹，它只要一出现就预示着天下太平。它身上的花纹象征着五种最珍贵的德行，头上花纹象征着品德，翅膀上的花纹象征着恭顺，背上的花纹象征着礼仪，肚子上的花纹象征着诚信，胸口上的花纹象征着仁爱。根据中国最古老的字典《尔雅》，凤凰是鸡头、燕颔、蛇颈、龟背、鱼尾，五彩色，高六尺许。凤凰的性格十分高洁，《庄子》中说，凤凰十分高贵，不是梧桐树的话就不在上面栖息，不是竹子的果实就不吃，不是清冽的甘泉就不喝。

凤凰的心地十分善良，它不啄食有生命的昆虫，也不伤害其他动物，更不会践踏有生命的花草，它被鸟类推选为鸟中之王。传说它每次飞翔之时，身边总是有百鸟相伴，场面十分壮观。每一年，所有的鸟还都要飞到凤凰那里去朝拜问候它。凤凰的鸣叫声也十分有特色，像音乐一样，时而激越昂扬，时而柔和悠长。在古代中国，就用"凤鸣"来形容最美妙的音乐。据说，中国的十二律，就是古人根据其鸣叫声创作出来的，古人有时会用这些美妙而高雅的乐曲吸引凤凰，如果音乐足够美，传说真的会有凤凰来听。

传说在东周时期，秦穆公有个美丽的女儿，名叫弄玉，她平时非常喜欢吹笙，而且技艺十分高超。在一个晚上，弄玉在睡梦之中看见一个英俊的男子从霞光灿烂的天空中飞下来，头上戴着羽冠，身上披着鹤

representing the majesty of the emperor. As dragons are deemed auspicious and festive, they can be seen everywhere in China. For instance, there are thousands of place names and over forty river names containing the Chinese character "long", which refers to the dragon. Dragon boats are rowed everywhere on the Dragon Boat Festival, dragon lanterns are appreciated all over the nation on the Lantern Festival, and dragon dance performances are dotted around the country in the streets and alleys on the Spring Festival. Moreover, the countless Dragon King Temples also serve to testify that the dragon has been carved into the bone marrow of the Chinese people.

According to the research conducted by some experts, the Chinese ancestors' dragon worship had a close relationship with agricultural production. In primitive society, agricultural harvest is directly related to water. In order to ensure favorable weather and a good harvest, the Chinese ancestors created the notion of the god in charge of rain—the dragon. Gradually, the dragon evolved into the spiritual sustenance of the Chinese people and the cultural belief of the Chinese nation. No matter where the Chinese people are, they can identify with each other as long as the dragon and dragon culture are mentioned. The majesty, supernatural power and sense of justice of the dragon embody the Chinese nation's spirits of self-esteem, confidence and unremitting self-improvement.

The Myth of the Chinese Phoenix

The Chinese phoenix is a kind of divine bird in ancient Chinese myths and legends, which makes its meaning differ from that of the phoenix in the West. It is born in the country of gentlemen in the East, and soars beyond the four seas. The advent of the phoenix will only occur on condition that the world is peaceful, the government politics is upright, and the country is prosperous. Therefore, after Dayu succeeded in taming the flood, there was a phoenix hovering in the sky. Confucius once complained that he did not live in a good time as there was no presence of the phoenix.

According to *The Classic of Mountains and Seas*, the phoenix grew in Danxue Mountain. In appearance, it is a bit like a rooster and has colorful stripes on its body. Its arrival heralds an era of peace. The patterns on its body symbolize

氅，身边跟着一只美丽的凤凰，他说："我是神山太华山的主人，请你和我结为夫妻吧！这是我们的缘分。"说完，便从腰间解下一支玉箫，凤凰闻箫声而翩翩起舞，时不时地发出鸣叫之声，凤声与箫声相和，犹如天籁。

第二天醒来，弄玉将梦中的事情告诉了父亲，秦穆公立刻命人前往太华山寻找那吹箫之人，过了几天，手下带回了一个叫萧史的年轻人。在大殿之上，萧史为众人表演吹箫，演奏第一曲时众人只觉清风习习，第二曲时彩云慢慢移动到了大殿的正上方，第三曲时白鹤成双成对地在空中飞翔，无数的孔雀飞到大殿中，百鸟和鸣。秦穆公惊喜万分，问萧史："这是怎么一回事？"萧史恭敬地回答道："箫声特别像凤凰的鸣叫，所以能将凤凰吸引而来，凤凰是百鸟之王，凤凰都来了，别的鸟自然也跟着飞来了。"

接下来，弄玉和萧史举行了盛大的婚礼，二人完婚后，日日笙箫相伴。过了大概半年之后，一天夜里，突然有一只通体金黄的凤，还有一只浑身赤红的龙出现在二人的面前，于是萧史骑赤龙、弄玉乘金凤，两人就此离开。之后很少有人再见到他们了，但两人因凤结缘的爱情故事却流传了下来，成为千古佳话。

凤和龙一样，都是中国特有的神话形象。一般来说，龙代表男性，凤代表女性。在封建社会，龙指代皇帝，凤指代皇后，龙凤在一起，就是至高无上的皇权的代名词。因此，在古代，只有皇后才能穿戴绣有凤凰样式的衣服和头饰。现如今，龙和凤成了年轻人结婚时常用的装饰形象，寓意着阴阳和谐、婚姻美满、吉祥如意。

the five most precious virtues. The patterns on its head stand for morality. Those on its wings represent obedience. Those on its back indicate etiquette. Those on its tummy embody honesty. Those on its chest stand for benevolence. It is recorded in China's oldest dictionary, *Erya*, that the phoenix appears with five colors on it; and the head of a chicken, the chin of a swallow, the neck of a snake, the back of a turtle, the tail of a fish. It is over six feet in height. The phoenix has a noble character. The classic book *Zhuangzi* has it that the phoenix is very high-minded—If it is not a plane tree, it will not perch on it. If it is not bamboo fruit, it will not eat it. If it is not a limpid spring, it will not drink it.

The phoenix has a golden heart. It never pecks at living insects, and neither does it harm other animals, nor trample on flowers or plants. The phoenix was elected by birds as their king. Legend has it that each time its flying, it is always accompanied by hundreds of birds, which constitutes a spectacular scene. Stories of the phoenix say that all the other birds would fly to pay homage to it annually. The chirping sound of the phoenix is also rather distinctive, just like music—sometimes stirring, sometimes soft and resounding. In ancient China, "the singing of the phoenix" was used to describe the most beautiful music. It is said that the twelve-tone equal temperament was composed by ancient Chinese people in accordance with the singing of the phoenix. They would sometimes play such beautiful and elegant music to attract the phoenix and the phoenix would indeed come to appreciate it only if the music was peerless enough.

It's said that during the Eastern Zhou Dynasty (770 BC-256 BC), Duke Mu of Qin had a pretty daughter named Nongyu, who was keen on playing the Sheng and was quite adroit in playing it. One night when Nongyu was sleeping, she saw a handsome man flying down from the rosy sky in her dream, wearing a feather crown and a cloak with a crane pattern. Accompanied by a gorgeous phoenix, the man said, "I am the master of the sacred Taihua Mountain. Please marry me. It's our fate." Then, he took a jade flute from his waist, and the phoenix danced trippingly upon hearing the sound of the flute. The phoenix sang from time to time, and its sound was in harmony with the sound of the flute, just like music from heaven.

The next day, Nongyu woke up and told her father about the dream. Duke Mu of Qin immediately ordered people to go to Taihua Mountain to find the

四灵神话

"四灵"指的是代表四方神灵的四种瑞兽,分别是青龙、白虎、朱雀、玄武。"四灵"又被称为"四神",青龙守护东方,白虎守护西方,朱雀守护南方,玄武守护北方;还管理着四季的运行,青龙主管春天,朱雀主管夏天,白虎主管秋天,玄武主管冬天。除此,"四灵"同时掌管着天上的二十八星宿,中国传统的二十八星宿,有点类似于西方天文学家说的星座,每一个星宿都由几颗或者几十颗数量不等的星星组成,"四灵"中的每一只神兽分别掌管七个星宿。可以发现,"四灵"分工合作,共同维护着天地之间的秩序和法则。

实际上,"四灵"都是中原地区先民的氏族图腾。青龙和白虎,顾名思义,就是青色的龙和白色的虎,龙在前文已经有过详细的介绍,虎

man who played the flute. A few days later, they brought back a young man named Xiao Shi, who then played the flute in the main hall of the palace. When he played the first song, everyone there felt a light breeze was blowing. When the second song was played, colorful clouds slowly approached the top of the hall. When the third song was played, white cranes were flying in pairs in the sky, countless peacocks flying into the hall, and all the birds were singing in chorus. Duke Mu of Qin was elated and asked Xiao Shi, "What is this?" Xiao Shi respectfully replied, "The sound of the flute is pretty like the sound of the phoenix, so it can attract it. The phoenix is the king of all birds. When the phoenix comes, other birds naturally follow."

Then, a grand wedding was held for Nongyu and Xiao Shi. After they got married, they played the Sheng and Xiao day after day. About half a year later, one night, a golden phoenix and a scarlet dragon appeared in front of them abruptly. Xiao Shi rode on the scarlet dragon, Nongyu rode on the golden phoenix, and they left. Few people ever saw them again, but their love story starting with a phoenix was handed down through the ages.

The Chinese phoenix together with the Chinese dragon is an exclusive mythological image in China. Generally speaking, the dragon represents the male and the phoenix represents the female. In feudal society, the dragon referred to the emperor and the phoenix to the empress. Together, the dragon and phoenix are synonymous with supreme imperial power. Due to this, in ancient times, only the empress could wear clothes and headdresses embroidered with phoenix patterns. Nowadays, the dragon and the phoenix are often used as decorative images for young people to use in the marriage ceremony, implying the harmony between Yin and Yang, a happy marriage and good luck.

The Myth of the Four Spirits

The Four Spirits refer to the four auspicious beasts representing the four deities in four directions. These are the Azure Dragon, the White Tiger, the Vermilion Bird and the Black Tortoise. The Four Spirits are also known as the Four Gods. The Azure Dragon guards the east; the White Tiger, the west; the Vermilion Bird, the south and the Black Tortoise, the north. They also manage

就是动物界中存在的老虎，在此不再赘述。朱雀的造型有点像孔雀，又有点像凤凰，整个身子如同一团永不熄灭的火焰。玄武是乌龟和蛇的结合体，玄指黑色，玄武指黑色的龟蛇。

  传说，尧舜时期，天下发起大洪水，为了保护百姓，"四灵"重现人间。据说，在人们即将被洪水卷走的时候，东方天空中蓦然出现一条身形矫健、闪闪发光的青龙；随后，西方天空中跃出一头张牙舞爪、怒目而视的白虎；南方天空中飞出一只羽毛鲜红放着金色光芒的大鸟；北方天空中爬出一只巨龟，身上还盘踞着一条黑蛇。它们气势非凡，一下子就镇住了趁洪水作恶的野兽，阻挡住了洪水的前进，随后大禹才能够专心致志地治理洪水。人们为了感谢"四灵"为百姓做出的贡献和牺牲，在人间为它们分别修建了庙宇，时时供奉，子子孙孙代代祭祀，从未间断。

  后来，这四种灵兽的图案被应用在了很多地方。例如，在行军打仗时，古人往往将其画在战旗之上，以此祈求"四灵"庇佑；在排兵布阵时，也常常使用"前朱雀、后玄武、左青龙、右白虎"的方法，不仅用其标明前后左右的军队位置，还用来振奋军威、鼓舞士气。再如，百姓们会在自己的房前屋后贴上绘有四灵画像的灵符，以此来镇降妖邪，保护自己家族的平安。到了现代，"四灵"的形象更是以标志、纹饰等形态频繁出现，这些形态经过现代人的再加工，更加符合现代人的审美，也更加丰富了"四灵"的文化内涵。

the running of the four seasons, with the Azure Dragon in charge of the spring; the Vermilion Bird, the summer; the White Tiger, the autumn; and the Black Tortoise, the winter. In addition, the Four Spirits also govern the twenty-eight constellations in the sky. The traditional Chinese twenty-eight constellations are somewhat similar to the constellations acknowledged by Western astronomers. Each constellation consists of several or dozens of stars. Each of the Four Spirits takes charge of seven constellations. They work in cooperation to maintain the order and laws between heaven and earth.

As a matter of fact, the Four Spirits were the clan totems of the Chinese ancestors in the Central Plains. The Azure Dragon and the White Tiger, as the names suggest, are a green dragon and a white tiger. The dragon has been introduced at length previously. The white tiger is the kind of tiger that exists in nature, so there is no need to give unnecessary details. The shape of the Vermilion Bird is a bit like a peacock as well as a phoenix, and its whole body resembles a flame that never goes out. The Black Tortoise is a combination of a turtle and a snake. It is called Xuanwu in Chinese with Xuan referring to the color black and Xuanwu indicating the black turtle and snake.

According to legend, during the period of Yao and Shun (around four thousand years ago), the world was once stricken by a deluge, and the Four Spirits appeared to salvage people. It is said that when the people were about to be swept away by the flood, a green dragon with a vigorous and gleaming body suddenly showing up in the eastern sky. Then, bearing its fangs, brandishing its claws and glaring at the flood. A white tiger jumped out from the western sky, a giant bird with vermilion feathers in golden light flew out from the southern sky, and an enormous tortoise with a black snake entwined on its body crawled out from the northern sky. They possessed such power and grandeur that they instantly quelled the beasts, who were taking advantage of the flood to do evil, and held back the advances of the flood. Only after this could Dayu commit himself to flood control. In order to thank the Four Spirits for their contributions and sacrifices to the common people, temples were built for them respectively and they were worshiped by one generation after another.

Later, the images of these four auspicious beasts were applied to various places. For example, during wartime, the ancient Chinese people would draw

精卫神话

传说在上古时代，北方有一座山叫发鸠山，山上有许多树。其中一棵树上有一只小鸟，这只小鸟的外形很像乌鸦，只是它的头上有红色的花纹，嘴巴是白色的，爪子是红色的，它的啼叫声好像在喊"精卫，精卫"，也是因为这个，人们都称它"精卫鸟"。

据说，精卫鸟原本是神农炎帝的小女儿，特别机灵可爱。当时中原地区的人们喜欢称呼没有成年的小女孩儿叫"娃"，所以大家都喜欢叫炎帝的这个小女儿为"女娃"。炎帝非常宠爱这个小女儿，可是因为他是部落首领，每天的工作都很多，除了要管理自己族群中的事务，还要整理大地上所有的五谷和药材。很多时候，女娃都见不到自己的父亲。

但是女娃却十分懂事，父亲没有时间陪她玩，她就自己一个人玩，常常头上插着一朵小花，有时奔跑在充满生机的田野中，有时去郁郁葱葱的树林中小憩，有时又会上山采些野花。这一天，女娃心血来潮，想去海边看一看，她一大清早就来到了东海的岸边，看着海的那一边，一轮朝阳慢慢地从东海升起，在海面上洒下无数的金光，真的是太美了！女娃兴奋极了，她情不自禁地跳入大海，朝着太阳的方向游去。她游啊游啊，最初她游得很欢快，很起劲，可是她游得越来越远，体力也渐渐耗尽……不知不觉，她游到了大海的深处。突然，海面上掀起了滔天巨浪，一个巨浪袭来，一下子把女娃卷入了深深的漩涡之中，女娃就这样丧命大海了。

可是谁也没想到，几天之后，一只小鸟在女娃沉没的地方破浪飞出，盘旋在东海的上空，发出"精卫、精卫"的悲鸣，据说这小鸟就是女娃的化身。人们根据她的叫声称呼她"精卫"。女娃因为痛恨无情的大海剥夺了自己的生命，心有不甘，在其死后，精魂化作一只小鸟，头上那朵鲜艳的小红花化作额头的花纹。为了向大海复仇，也为了不再让

them on the army flags to pray for their blessings. When arranging troops, the lineup followed this pattern: the Vermilion Bird in the front, the Black Tortoise in the back, the Azure Dragon in the left and the White Tiger in the right. This lineup was often employed, which was not only used to pinpoint the positions of the troops in the front, back, left, and right, but also to boost the military's prestige and morale. Moreover, the people would stick talismans with images of the Four Spirits on the front and back of their houses so as to suppress evil spirits and safeguard their families. In modern times, the images of the Four Spirits have gained in popularity in the forms of signs and ornaments. These reprocessed forms are more in line with a modern aesthetic point of view and have also enriched the cultural connotation of the Four Spirits.

The Myth of Jingwei

Legend has it that in immemorial times, there was a mountain in the north called Fajiu Mountain, on which there were plenty of trees. On one of the trees, there was a little bird, which looked like a crow, but had red patterns on its head, a white mouth and red claws. It was because its twittering sounded like "Jingwei, Jingwei" that people called it the Jingwei bird.

It is said that the Jingwei bird was originally the youngest daughter of Shennong, the Yan Emperor, and she was particularly smart and adorable. At that time, people in the Central Plains used to call underage little girls "Wa", so everyone liked to call the youngest daughter of the Yan Emperor "Nüwa"(meaning the little girl). The Yan Emperor loved the little girl a lot. However, as a tribal leader, he had much work to deal with. In addition to managing the tribal affairs, he also needed to sort out all the grains and medical materials on the earth. Thus, for most of the time, the little girl did not see her father.

Nevertheless, the girl was not self-willed at all. If her father had no time to play with her, she would play alone, often with a flower on her head. She would sometimes run in the vibrant fields, go to the lush woods for a nap, or pick some wild flowers on the mountain. One day, on a whim, the girl felt like going to the beach for sightseeing. She reached the shore of the Eastern Sea early in the morning. Looking at the other side of the sea, she saw the sun was slowly rising

更多的人被大海吞噬生命,她下定决心,不管用多长时间,都要将东海填平。

从此,精卫鸟就住在布满荆棘的发鸠山上,每天天不亮,就衔着小石头或者小树枝,飞到东海的上空,往东海里扔,然后再回到发鸠山去衔新的小石头和树枝。如此成年累月,往复飞翔,从不停歇。大海不停地奔腾着,咆哮着,似乎是在嘲笑精卫的自不量力,可是精卫却不在乎,它还是不断地做着重复的工作,无论阴晴风雨。

东海终于忍不住了,它问:"你为什么一天又一天地往我身上扔石头、树枝?"

精卫说:"因为你夺走了我的生命,我要向你报仇。"

东海不屑地说道:"报仇就这么重要吗?你这又是何苦?"

精卫顿时激动了起来:"我不只是为了我自己,更是为了让你再也无法吞噬无辜的生命。"

大海疯狂地呼啸着:"那你就填吧,可是傻鸟儿,就算再过一千年一万年,你都休想将我填平,不过是白白浪费时间。"

"不,我要填,我要一千年一万年地填下去,哪怕到宇宙的尽头,哪怕世界末日,只要我永不放弃,总有一天我会把你填平的。"精卫坚定地回答道,说完,它又飞回发鸠山,去衔石头和树枝了。

天神听说了精卫鸟填海的事情,十分感动,为了帮助精卫,他将黄土高原上的泥沙卷起来投入东海,海水瞬间被大量的泥沙搅黄了,所以,人们才会将被黄沙侵染的东海北部称为"黄海"。眼看着自己有被填平的危险,东海害怕了,它赶紧采取措施,开始拼命地将泥沙、石头和树枝推向海岸,这些东西在海岸边不断地沉淀堆积下来,形成一片片浅滩,浅滩慢慢地变厚变宽,人们将其开垦,改造成良田。

精卫填海的故事流传了下来,精卫鸟锲而不舍的坚定意志和虽弱小却敢于跟强大势力抗争的不屈不挠的精神,鼓励着一代又一代的中华儿女奋勇前行,精卫填海的精神成了中华民族最重要的精神品质之一。

above the sea level and the seawater was glittering, which constituted a splendid scene. The girl was so fascinated that she instantly jumped into the sea and swam towards the sun. In the beginning, she swam merrily and vigorously, but as she went farther and farther, she gradually became exhausted. Before she realized it, she had swum too far from shore. Suddenly, a huge wave broke out on the sea, which hit her and trapped the little girl in a deep whirlpool. The little girl then lost her life to the sea.

However, no one had ever expected that a few days later, a bird flew out of the place where the little girl was drowned, hovered over the Eastern Sea, and uttered a mournful cry of "Jingwei, Jingwei". It's said that this bird was the little girl and people called her Jingwei because of her twittering. The little girl hated the merciless sea bitterly for depriving her of her life. So, filled with indignation, her spirit transformed into a bird after her death and the bright red flower on her head turned into a pattern on its forehead. In order to take revenge on the sea and in order that no more people would be swallowed up by it, Jingwei was determined to fill up the Eastern Sea no matter how long it would take.

The legends say that the Jingwei bird lived on Fajiu Mountain, which was full of thorns. Every day before dawn, Jingwei would fly to the Eastern Sea and throw the small stones and twigs in its mouth into the sea. Then it would come back to the mountain again to carry other stones and twigs, back and forth, doing so for ages without a stop. The sea kept seething and roaring as if mocking Jingwei's overreaching itself. Jingwei never cared, but constantly practiced its repetitive work, no matter what the weather was like.

Finally, the Eastern Sea couldn't bear it anymore and asked, "Why are you throwing stones and twigs at me day after day?"

Jingwei remarked, "Because you have taken my life, I will take my revenge on you."

The Eastern Sea said disdainfully, "What's the point of revenge? Why do you bother?"

Jingwei suddenly became agitated and said, "I do it not for myself, but also for any innocent lives you can never devour."

The sea roared frantically, "Then just do it, but silly bird, even in another thousand or ten thousand years, you will never fill me up. It is nothing but a waste

第六章 灵怪神话

of time."

"Yes, I will do it. I will do it for a thousand years and even for ten thousand years, even if it reaches the end of the universe, even if the world ends. As long as I never give up, I will fill you up one day." Jingwei firmly replied, and as it finished talking, it flew back to the Fajiu Mountain to pick up stones and twigs.

The God of Heaven heard about the story of Jingwei and was quite moved by it. To assist Jingwei, he swept up the sediment on the Loess Plateau and poured it into the Eastern Sea. The sea water was instantly turned yellow because of the sediment. Therefore, the northern part of the Eastern Sea mixed with the yellow sand was called the Yellow Sea. Seeing that it was in danger of being filled up, the Eastern Sea was frightened. Thus, it took swift measures and began to desperately push sand, stones and twigs toward the shore. These deposits accumulated along the coast, forming shallow banks, which gradually became thick and wide, and were then cultivated and converted into fertile fields by people.

The story of Jingwei trying to fill the sea has been handed down in China. The perseverance of the Jingwei bird and its dauntless spirit of fighting against a strong power despite being small and weak have inspired generations of Chinese people to forge ahead and it has become one of the most significant spiritual qualities of the Chinese nation.

后记

本书中所选取的神话故事在中国几乎家喻户晓，是每个孩子幼时的启蒙故事。在流传过程中，基本每一个神话故事都有不同的版本，情节也越来越复杂，我们选取的是流传较广、趣味性较强的版本，并进行了简单化、故事化的通俗演绎描述。

中原神话中的每一位神仙、每一位精灵都充满了人性。他们有着勇敢无畏、心地善良的美好人性，也像普通人一样会表现出忧伤、愤怒或怯懦的情绪，他们就像我们身边的朋友，讲述着他们的故事，传递着他们的喜怒哀乐。强大而温柔的女娲是我们对母亲的投影；智慧而富有领导能力的伏羲更像是一位理想的父亲；黄帝在战场上呼风唤雨的英勇身影令人激动难忘；奔向月亮的嫦娥展示了追求自由的力量；而夸父和精卫，一个不顾一切奔向太阳，一个以微小之躯发誓填平大海，他们虽然力量弱小，看起来在做着傻事，却位列中国人最受喜爱的神灵之中，因为他们为了梦想不懈追求，哪怕生命的停止都不能熄灭这熊熊燃烧的理想之光。无数中国人在生活的至暗时刻，就会情不自禁地想到夸父和精卫，想到勇敢盗取火种的阏伯，想到死后也不忘战斗的共工，想到手持长剑英勇战斗的黑衣玄女，或是象征光明与爱情的洛水女神。这些来自遥远时代的神祇此刻就像在脆弱人们的身边，轻声讲述自己的故事，鼓励人们重新振作，对理想不轻言放弃。世世代代，中国的孩子在聆听这些故事的时候，不仅可以被有趣的情节吸引，而且可以学会如何做一个善良、勇敢、真诚的人，了解自己的祖先在中原莽莽大地上的筚路蓝缕之功。神话是每一个民族的宝贵精神财富，彰显着传承不息的民族精

Epilogue

The myths and stories selected in this book are almost household names in China, and they are the enlightenment stories to the delight of every child. During the process of transmission, different versions for almost every story arose, and the plots became more and more complicated. The stories chosen here are the ones that are widely accepted and are among the more entertaining versions that appeared after a series of simplified, fictionalized and popular description and narration.

Every immortal and every spirit in the myths of the Central Plains is represented as having a full display of the characteristics of human nature. They not only embody noble humanity like courage and kindness, but also they show sadness, anger and cowardice, just like common people. They resemble our friends, telling their stories and sharing their joys and sorrows. The mighty but gentle Nüwa is our projection of a mother. Fuxi, with his wisdom and leadership, is more like an ideal father. The heroic figure of the Yellow Emperor on the battlefield is heartening and unforgettable. Chang'e, who flew to the moon, displays the strength of pursuing freedom. As for Kuafu and Jingwei, one desperately chased after the sun, and the other vowed to fill up the sea despite having a tiny body. Weak and even seemingly foolish as they are, they are among the most beloved gods in China because of their relentless pursuit of their dreams and also because even the cessation of life they cannot extinguish the flame of their ideals. In the darkest moments of their lives, myriads of Chinese people would spontaneously recall Kuafu, Jingwei, and Ebo who bravely stole fire, Gonggong who never forgot to fight after his demise, Xuannü in black who fought heroically with a long sword and the goddess of Luoshui who symbolized brightness and love. These gods from immemorial times appear to be at the side of vulnerable people at the moment, whispering about their stories, encouraging the people to strive harder and not to abandon their ideals easily. From one generation to another, when Chinese

神。希望每一位读者都能喜欢这些小故事，可以从中了解到一些发祥于中原地区的中华文明，或者被故事中一个个鲜活的中国神明与精灵感动和激励。

children listen to these stories, they not only are captivated by the fascinating plots, but also learn how to be someone kind, brave and sincere, understanding the hardships and achievements of their ancestors in the wild land of the Central Plains. Myths are the precious spiritual wealth of every nation, reflecting the ceaseless inheritance of the national spirit. It's hoped that every reader will enjoy these short stories, gain some insights into the Chinese civilization originated in the Central Plains, and be touched and inspired by the vivid Chinese immortals and spirits in the stories.

附录：中国历史年代简表
Appendix: A Brief Chronology of Chinese History

中国历史年代简表
A Brief Chronology of Chinese History

五帝时代 Period of the Five Legendary Rulers c. 2600 BC–c. 2070 BC	黄帝 Huangdi (Yellow Emperor)	
	颛顼 Zhuanxu	
	帝喾 Diku (Emperor Ku)	
	尧 Yao	
	舜 Shun	
夏 Xia Dynasty	c. 2070 BC–c. 1600 BC	
商 Shang Dynasty	c. 1600 BC–c. 1046 BC	
西周 Western Zhou Dynasty	c. 1046 BC–c. 771 BC	
东周 Eastern Zhou Dynasty 770 BC–256 BC	春秋 Spring and Autumn Period	770 BC–476 BC
	战国 Warring States Period	475 BC–221 BC
秦 Qin Dynasty	221 BC–206 BC	
汉 Han Dynasty 206 BC–220 AD	西汉 Western Han	206 BC–25 AD
	东汉 Eastern Han	25 AD–220 AD
三国 Three Kingdoms 220 AD–280 AD	魏 Wei	220 AD–265 AD
	蜀汉 Shu Han	221 AD–263 AD
	吴 Wu	222 AD–280 AD
晋 Jin Dynasty 265 AD–420 AD	西晋 Western Jin	265 AD–317 AD
	东晋 Eastern Jin	317 AD–420 AD

续表 Continued Table

南北朝 Southern and Northern Dynasties 420 AD-589 AD	南朝 Southern Dynasties	宋 Song	420 AD-479 AD
		齐 Qi	479 AD-502 AD
		梁 Liang	502 AD-557 AD
		陈 Chen	557 AD-589 AD
	北朝 Northern Dynasties	北魏 Northern Wei	386 AD-534 AD
		东魏 Eastern Wei	534 AD-550 AD
		北齐 Northern Qi	550 AD-577 AD
		西魏 Western Wei	535 AD-556 AD
		北周 Northern Zhou	557 AD-581 AD
隋 Sui Dynasty		581 AD-618 AD	
唐 Tang Dynasty		618 AD-907 AD	
五代十国 Five Dynasties and Ten States	五代 Five Dynasties 907 AD-960 AD	后梁 Later Liang	907 AD-923 AD
		后唐 Later Tang	923 AD-936 AD
		后晋 Later Jin	936 AD-947 AD
		后汉 Later Han	947 AD-950 AD
		后周 Later Zhou	951 AD-960 AD
	十国 Ten States 902 AD-979 AD	北汉 Northern Han	951 AD-979 AD
		吴 Wu	902 AD-937 AD
		吴越 Wuyue	907 AD-978 AD
		闽 Min	909 AD-945 AD
		南汉 Southern Han	917 AD-971 AD
		荆南（又称"南平"）Jingnan (Nanping)	924 AD-963 AD
		楚 Chu	927 AD-951 AD
		南唐 Southern Tang	937 AD-975 AD
		前蜀 Former Shu	907 AD-925 AD
		后蜀 Later Shu	934 AD-965 AD

续表 Continued Table

宋 Song Dynasty 960 AD-1279 AD	北宋 Northern Song	960 AD-1127 AD
	南宋 Southern Song	1127 AD-1279 AD
辽 Liao (契丹 Qidan/Khitan)	907 AD-1125 AD	
西夏 Xixia (Tangut)	1038 AD-1227 AD	
金 Jin	1115 AD-1234 AD	
元 Yuan Dynasty	1206 AD-1368 AD	
明 Ming Dynasty	1368 AD-1644 AD	
清 Qing Dynasty	1616 AD-1911 AD	
中华民国 Republic of China	1912 AD-1949 AD	
中华人民共和国 People's Republic of China	1949 AD-	